DOING GOOD

Doing Good

Racial Tensions and Workplace Inequalities at a Community Clinic in El Nuevo South

NATALIA DEEB-SOSSA

THE UNIVERSITY OF
ARIZONA PRESS
TUCSON

THE UNIVERSITY OF ARIZONA PRESS

www.uapress.arizona.edu

Library of Congress Cataloging-in-Publication Data
Deeb-Sossa, Natalia.
    Doing good : racial tensions and workplace inequalities at a community clinic in El Nuevo South / Natalia Deeb-Sossa.
        pages cm
    Includes bibliographical references and index.
    ISBN 978-0-8165-2132-6 (cloth : alk. paper) 1. Social status—Health aspects—North Carolina. 2. Equality—Health aspects—North Carolina. 3. Community health services—North Carolina—Employees. 4. Discrimination in employment. 5. Hispanic Americans—North Carolina. I. Title.
    RA418.5.S63D44 2013
    331.7'61362109756—dc23
                                                                    2012030853

Publication of this book is made possible in part by the proceeds of a permanent endowment created with the assistance of a Challenge Grant from the National Endowment for the Humanities, a federal agency.

Manufactured in the United States of America on acid-free, archival-quality paper containing a minimum of 30% post-consumer waste and processed chlorine free.

18 17 16 15 14 13   6 5 4 3 2 1

Well, believe it or not, I was sitting in church one Monday night and I had been praying about a job, been praying and been praying for a clinical job. This is something I've always wanted to do, was work in the clinic. I always wanted to work with babies. Really with people, but babies particularly. So, one Monday night at church I didn't cut my cell phone off. I normally do. My cell phone rung and it was a friend of mine called me and says "Look, I got a phone call from a friend saying her friend has a job opening where she worked at. If you want the job, you need to go." And that's how I got the job. . . . I got the call that Monday night. I was there on the Tuesday and hired on Tuesday. . . . And where I work at it's mostly Latino, Spanish-speaking people. I do not speak Spanish, but I understand it very well. And I still enjoy working with them. A lot of the patients there now have gotten comfortable with me and they know that I don't speak it. So, it still makes it all good. Yeah. . . . And it's a good place to come to because our doctors are very good. They're very good doctors to work for. . . . I think the clinic is a good clinic. A lot of people that doesn't have the money, that can't afford it, [the clinic] helps those people and I think that's a wonderful thing. It's a wonderful thing to work here and be a part of this.

—*From an interview with African American Medical Assistant (II), "Eva"*

Contents

Illustrations

Acknowledgments

Comunidad (community) and *amistad* (friendship) helped me bring this book to completion. It has been a long haul, and I am grateful to all who have supported me all these years converting my dissertation research into a publishable manuscript. ¡Mil Gracias!

My deep thanks go to Sherryl Kleinman, my advisor and dissertation chair, for her insights, conscientiousness in reading and commenting on numerous drafts, and mentorship while I was a graduate student at the University of North Carolina at Chapel Hill. I am indebted to Krista McQueeney, Matt Ezzell, and Ken Kolb for their unflagging support and valuable feedback and editing on the multiple drafts of my dissertation. I am also grateful to Heather Kane and Michael Schwalbe for their insightful comments on drafts of my dissertation, and to LeAnna Lang for her transcription assistance and continued friendship. I also want to thank my committee members, Karen M. Booth, Kathleen Harris, Karolyn Tyson, and Thomas Konrad for their guidance, support, and feedback.

I am also grateful to Vicki Smith, Carole Joffe, Diane Wolf, and Jennifer Bickham-Mendez for the detailed and thoughtful feedback that they offered on earlier versions of this book. I also want to thank the faculty and staff of the Chicana/o Studies Department at the University of California at Davis for their mentorship, support, and colleagueship, from which I have benefited much. Gracias Adela, Miroslava, Yvette, Angie, Sergio, Malaquias, Carlos, Maceo, Gloria, Kevin, Osa Bear, Alma, Roxana, Kathy, Letty, and Alyssa.

In addition, I want to thank Acquiring Editor Kristen Buckles at the University of Arizona Press and the three anonymous reviewers for the time and resources they invested in this book. The book is stronger than it was before the review process. I also want to thank John Sullivan and Susan Campbell for their help in editing.

Many thanks to the staff and clients of Care Inc. for their trust and for letting me hang around for a year and a half; gracias for their generosity and willingness to share their experiences with me.

Finally, I dedicate this book to my family, my first teachers. They have always supported me in my daily struggles for justice, dignity, and universal health care. This book is for you, Mom (Clara Inés), Dad (Alejandro Mauricio), Gelica (my sister), Abuelita Ana María (grandmother), Tío Julio Ricardo (uncle), and all my other family in Colombia too extensive to list. This book is also dedicated to my adoptive family here in the United States: Caleb, Adriana Elisa, Fred, Erna, Melissa, Steve, Ixchel, Ruby, Orion, Rick, Donna, Badiah, Gloria, Rosana, Kerry, Lori, and Cayce, whose daily examples of courage gave me the confidence to finish this project.

DOING GOOD

1

Introduction

Meaningful Work and
Moral Identity

IN THE FOLLOWING ANALYSIS of the construction and maintenance of "moral identity" (Kleinman 1996) by health-care providers at a community clinic in North Carolina (pseudonymously referred to as "Care Inc."), I explore the ways that workers' race, class, gender, and nationality shape their fashioning of a superior self-image. I examine how workers, like Eva above, construct a moral identity in the context of reconfigured race relations resulting from rapid Latina/o immigration to North Carolina, a new destination for these people. The mobilization of Mexican immigrants and other Latinas/os in sizable numbers to North Carolina altered the white–African American racial proportion of the state, transformed the ethnic makeup of social classes (in particular the working class of North Carolina), changed local politics, and affected both public and private institutional dynamics as organizations incorporated newcomers (Zúñiga and Hernández-León 2005). The arrival of Mexicans and other Latinas/os also transformed what Zúñiga and Hernández-León call "the symbolic definition of receiving localities," as Catholicism, Spanish language, Latina/o music, and Latina/o cuisine became part of public spaces (i.e., shopping centers, street corners, and commercial storefronts) and of the region's socioeconomic landscape. The presence of these newcomers created interethnic and linguistic tensions—as residents and public officials discussed the pros and

1

cons of bilingual education—as well as economic tensions and new economic dynamics, through the rise of immigrant entrepreneurship (187–274).

Throughout this book I address the question: How do workers maintain a sense of value about their work while long-standing race relations are reconfigured in the context of hyper-immigration? I highlight the dynamic nature of racialized relations, as well as the gender-based, class-based, and citizenship-based systems of oppression that shape the construction and maintenance of the health-care providers' moral identity. For the health-care providers at Care Inc., the worth of Care Inc.—and their worth as health-care workers—depended on whether they believed they were "doing something good," a phrase I heard repeatedly throughout my research. But there were different definitions for "doing good" and different moral foundations underlying those definitions, depending on the workers' gender, class, race/ethnicity, and citizenship status. Most importantly, these health-care providers failed to see how, in constructing and maintaining their own positive moral identity, they were led to treat each other and their patients unequally, and thus to contradict their ideals of doing good. Furthermore, the staffers denied that the ways they acted had hurtful consequences or reinforced race, class, and gender inequality. As Kleinman (1996, 11) writes, "We become so invested in our belief in ourselves as . . . 'good people' that we cannot see the reactionary or hurtful consequences of our behaviors."

Meaningful work can aid in safeguarding a positive moral identity. Analyzing how workers maintain a sense of value about their work, despite difficult working conditions, falls in the tradition of Everett C. Hughes (1958, 1971) and the Chicago School of Sociology.

For example, Joffe (1978) found that abortion counselors at Urban Clinic, a private nonprofit family planning agency, wanted their clients to perceive and acknowledge abortion as morally problematic, something that clients were less and less willing to do. The clients' behavior was important to counselors because they felt ambivalent about abortion: they were pro-choice, but their involvement in the abortion process became troubling to them. Joffe found that clients' attitudes, in large part, determined whether counselors experienced their work as "heroic" or "suspect." Counselors were more likely to see their work as suspect when counseling cynical or detached women, hostile clients, and women who acted bored when discussing future contraceptive plans.

In her later work, Joffe (1986) analyzed how birth control and abortion counselors at a women's health clinic responded to difficult working conditions. The administrators of the clinic saw counseling as time-consuming and expensive, and as a potential Pandora's box, because the clinic would have to provide for all clients' needs. Counselors used coping strategies to deal with their highly intense and low-paying jobs, including being pro-natalist. To avoid presenting an anti-natalist image, abortion-clinic employees gave pregnant staffers special attention.

Others document how difficult it is for abortion providers to feel good about their work. Simonds (1996) found that workers had difficulty assisting in second-trimester abortions. These health-care workers questioned why women would wait so long. Yet these providers' strong belief in a woman's right to choose to have an abortion (even a late one) helped them come to terms with and justify what they did on the job.

Even in "moral" work, such as volunteering at a homeless shelter, certain conditions can threaten volunteers' positive sense of self. Holden (1997, 125) found that one shelter's hierarchy and job requirements diminished the volunteers' sense of moral integrity. Managers instructed volunteers to "spy on," "tell on," and "order around" guests in the shelters. According to Holden, "the more rigorously the volunteers acted in their capacity as rule enforcers and shelter functionaries, the more likely it was that the guests would show hostility toward them." Volunteers fashioned a moral identity as "egalitarian" by acting as friends to guests and enforcing rules at their discretion. Their success at feeling egalitarian depended on their ability to pretend that they were unaware of the status differences between themselves and their clients.

In a related vein, Stein (1989) found that volunteers in soup kitchens and food pantries expected their clients to express at least benign neutrality, and preferably thankfulness, toward them. Clients' expressions of gratitude confirmed the volunteers' generosity and their self-concept as caring people. Clients' expressions of anger, hostility, arrogance, defiance, or resentment challenged volunteers' beliefs that they were doing good work.

Allahyari (2000) explored how people develop "moral selves" through acts of service to the needy and how an organization's "vision of charity" informs both the type of services offered to their guests and also the way the staff and volunteers view their own activities. Allahyari studied two Sacramento religious organizations, the Catholic Loaves and Fishes and the Salvation Army Shelter Service Center. The largely white, female, middle-class workers at Loaves and Fishes were committed to helping the poorest and most helpless of society and were dedicated to making the larger society more just and equitable. They worked under the assumption that each guest, no matter how apparently unappealing, ungrateful, and unworthy, was an ambassador of God. Each guest was to be welcomed as an equal and as a soul of incalculable value. The most difficult aspect of this work, according to the Loaves and Fishes volunteers, was overcoming their tendency to judge the poor as inferior and to withdraw from them. The Salvation Army, on the other hand, worked for the salvation of the "sinking classes" by strongly emphasizing the duty of each individual client to take responsibility for bettering himself or herself. As a result, the organization stressed hierarchy and the moral boundary between the clients and those who cared for them. The majority of the workers at the Salvation Army were "drafted volunteers," who were performing mandated community service under California's Alternative Sentencing Program, or who were residents of the center's "in-house" shelter. The majority of these drafted volunteers were working-class males, often non-white; a significant percentage of the staffers had themselves once been clients at the center, and these men served as role models for the drafted volunteers. Paradoxically, the staff and volunteers were actually close to the poor they served, making it difficult to establish and maintain the hierarchy and boundary between staff and clients that the organization valued.

In spite of challenges, some workers constructed a positive self-image, a "moral identity" (Kleinman 1996) that helped them persevere under difficult circumstances. These workers believe they are good people because they think their deeds and responses are consistent with that identity. Kleinman (5) defines "moral identity" as: "An identity that people invest with moral significance; our belief in ourselves as good people depends on whether we think our actions and reactions are consistent with that identity. By this definition, any identity that testifies to a person's good character can be a moral identity, such as mother, Christian, breadwinner, or feminist."

Sociologists have studied identity—the meanings through which we and others define ourselves—since the 1930s. For interactionists, identities are not set; they are socially constructed and shaped by life's social and cultural conditions (Blumer 1969; Mead 1934). Different groups (e.g., Latina; woman; foreign born; sociologist; recovering Catholic; single; queer identified) and different positions and roles in these groups create differences in identities. These identities are shaped by and reshape the world around us, and they impact how we interpret it (Blumer). They are performed, constructed, and negotiated in everyday social interactions (Goffman 1959; McCall and Simmons 1978) and may vary over time and place. Individuals create identity as they create new meanings, behaviors, and organizational arrangements through individual or joint action. These identities, altered and refined through interaction with others, have social and material consequences (Howard 2000).

Feminists of color have called attention to the need to understand how numerous identities—race, ethnicity, gender, class, and nationality—are experienced in daily life and how these identities intersect with and shape each other. Intersectional feminist theorists argue that identities are shaped by the multiple, interconnected, oppressed and privileged groups we belong to (Anzaldúa and Moraga 2002). As Collins (2000, 11) explains, intersectional theorists "view race, class, gender, sexuality, ethnicity, and age, among others, as mutually constructing systems of power. [And] . . . these systems permeate all social relations."

Mies (1986, 6–14), for example, noted the importance of taking into account the divisions among women to understand how those living under patriarchy also have cultural, social, economic, and political circumstances that differentiate their experience of sexism from that of other women. Mies argued that these divisions are found not only in different sets of women separated along national, class, race, or ethnic lines, but also within sets of women in the same category.

Intersectional theory calls upon interactionists to study moral identity to analyze how individuals' positions within multiple interlocking systems of inequality shape their identities and their construction of a moral identity (Roth 2004). In my analysis, I highlight how inter-sectionality works "on the ground" and plays out in the everyday interactions of these workers.

Building on Anzaldúa's conceptualization of "borderlands," I analyze how "borders" of social membership are constructed and enforced in "el Nuevo South." Anzaldúa's *Borderlands/La Frontera* (1987, 1) highlights the changing consciousness (what Anzaldúa describes as "perspective from the cracks") of those who reside in la frontera. The border is "'una herida abierta' where the Third World grates against the first and bleeds" (25) and "the lifeblood of two worlds" merges "to form a third—a border culture" (3). Borderlands are sites that enable people to negotiate the contradictions and ten-sions found in diverse cultural, class, and other forms of differences. Anzaldúa writes of the diversity of cross-border migrants and border dwellers, and the painful process associated with mestiza conscious-ness in her poems, including "Sus plumas el viento," "Sobrepiedras con lagaritjos," and "El sonavebitch." She understands that not all border crossers and border dwellers develop similar analyses of their experiences and social location.

Drawing on data collected from a year and a half of participant observation and interviews at Care Inc., I illustrate how an inter-sectional perspective deepens our understanding of moral identity: in this case, the moral identity of health-care providers who worked with the underserved in North Carolina. These health-care provid-ers crafted a moral identity by drawing on ways of understanding and knowing—the "cultural toolkit" (Swidler 1986)—or on cul-tural resources (Einwohner, Hollander, and Olson 2000; Williams 1995) available to them. Each group used these cultural resources for "claims-making activities" (Holstein and Miller 1993; Schneider 1985) and for developing credible rhetoric (Pedriana and Stryker 1997) regarding controversial issues. Claims-making is successful, in part, to the extent that framing of issues (Goffman 1974) builds upon a "stock of folk ideas and beliefs" (Snow and Benford 1988, 204).

Analyzing cultural resources (Einwohner, Hollander, and Olson 2000; Williams 1995) and constructing moral identity are important for understanding the world and for building movements (Scott 1998; Taylor 1999). In her study of the postpartum depression self-help movements, Taylor highlights the extent to which gender—images of femininity and masculinity—are reproduced in the language used by members of these self-help movements to frame their activism. As Taylor (21) notes, "[t]he language of gender difference and power is pervasive in contemporary women's self-help and serves as a major framework for understanding the problems that trouble women."

In her study of two feminist organizations, West Coast Women and El Refugio, Scott (1998, 409) explores how categories of racial-ethnic identity are constructed and how women negotiate the complexity of racial-ethnic identity in alliance-building in the day-to-day reality of feminist activism. Scott highlights how the members/activists, in their daily work of providing services to battered women and rape victims, began to "deconstruct the essentialism" of the discursive scripts and challenge the validity of their preconceived ideas that categorized "whites" as potentially racist and "people of color" as probable allies. Scott concludes that the scripts used by activists "are not so self-consciously created [and] such scripts are emerging in sites of grassroots feminism as well."

Kleinman, in her ethnography of the alternative health-care center Renewal (1996), found that the men practitioners were at the top, while the staff and volunteer women were at the bottom, of what was supposed to be a nonhierarchical organization. The men at Renewal had most of the power and influence and were revered by the staff and volunteer women. These women were grateful to have the opportunity to care for and work under the men, who benefited from these arrangements. Kleinman found that inequities were masked, in part, because members shared a moral identity that made them feel good about themselves. All members of Renewal shared a vision and a mission. Their shared racial and class identities also helped them maintain their moral identity. All of the practitioners and staff were white and had access to middle-class resources (their sacrifices for the organization were a conscious decision that could be reconsidered if need be). Kleinman concludes that the (white) men "saw themselves as having transcended the divisions created by gender, credentials, and social class. . . . But . . . social and economic arrangements . . . as well as ingrained ideas about gender and credentials led members to treat each other unequally" (124).

Similarly, Schwalbe (1996) examines how men in the mythopoetic movement—a self-help group that critically interpreted fairy tales as a tool for personal insight—tried to fashion the concept of "man" as a moral identity, but in the process they drew upon and reinforced the ideology of male supremacy. Heath, in her study of men in the Promise Keepers movement (2003), examines how their identities promote and/or impede social change. She also explores how race, class, gender, and sexual orientation shape identities in the movement. Heath uses Taylor and Whittier's conceptualization of collective identities (1992), which lists three factors—boundaries, consciousness, and negotiation—that shape the formation of identity within groups, such as the Promise Keepers movement, that have contradictory gender and racial ideologies. Heath's study shows how this movement fosters men's growth by encouraging them to embrace a caring and expressive masculinity, while reinforcing the gender and racial privilege accorded white men (439–442).

Scott's study of two activist organizations (2000), El Refugio and West Coast Women, examined how understandings of racism and activist practices "emerge as a product of what social movement actors do in their pursuit of social change" (785). Members of El Refugio and West Coast Women articulated and integrated two different understandings of racism: a structural view of racism as well as an individual view of racism. As Scott notes (812–13): "By deploying both meanings of racism, these actors implicitly refused the historic dichotomy that has characterized these approaches. In their actions, they suggested that racism is both a matter of face-to-face interaction, beliefs, and attitudes, as well as a matter of structures of power and inequality." Scott explains that activists both express values using the worldviews available to them and create alternative meanings as they address racism and racial representation within their organizations and within the services provided to rape victims and battered women:

> Human beings (and the groups they form) are not entirely self-defining agents or purely rational actors. . . . [T]hey are strategic actors loosely guided by the schemas relevant to their cultural context and structural location. Movements and activists are both the products of culture and the creators of culture. They express the values and beliefs of their cultural contexts, as well as perform the rituals and practices available therein. Activists choose from what Ann Swidler calls a "toolkit" of available worldviews and ways of doing things when they define problems and construct strategies of action. They do not create meanings and practices entirely anew, but rather to do so are both

constrained and enabled by the cultural and structural resources available to them in a particular historical moment. However, activists in social movement contexts are also "knowledgeable" agents who take informed action based on shared understandings of intended outcome. Their "knowledge" derives from the cultural milieu, but it can be used in creative ways. . . . They interpret and use the cultural resources available to them, and perhaps transform them. (787)

The new understandings of racism, Scott explains, are an unintended consequence of the anti-racist activists' actions (813). Maintaining a moral identity often involves perpetuating racist concepts, even subconsciously or in the guise of upholding some other ideal.

In like manner, Bonilla-Silva (2003) understands racism to be systemic and institutionalized. Racism, Bonilla-Silva contends, is not mere individual prejudice. Race is a constructed social category, which, in turn, produces a racialized social structure that promotes and reinforces white privilege. The racialized social structure, Bonilla-Silva argues, is maintained and reproduced by racial ideologies that legitimize and justify the racial status quo (8–11). One important racial ideology that promotes and reinforces racism is what Bonilla-Silva calls "colorblind racism."

Bonilla-Silva draws attention to the way many US citizens, in particular whites, avoid talking about race and racism by using colorblind language, dismissing race and the racism that bubbles underneath. He describes the hostility toward African Americans felt by many (perhaps most) whites, due in large part to the severe misunderstanding of, distance from, and animosity toward African Americans on the part of those whites. He contends that the façade of colorblindness defends anti–African American racism using colorblind language, which takes different forms. Colorblind language includes the use of and attachment to historically American ideals such as meritocracy, individuality, and choice (which Bonilla-Silva labels as "abstract liberalism"); the belief that racial segregation is a "natural" occurrence and not a result of history, politics, or culture (which he classifies as "naturalization"); the belief that others are culturally deficient or have a cultural deficient mode of thinking ("cultural racism"); and the belief that racism is no longer a strong influence on the lives of people of color ("minimization of racism"). Understanding these interrelated components of colorblind racism, Bonilla-Silva contends, enables us to analyze different manifestations of racism and work toward challenging them. The construction of moral identity often falls back on racist notions: privileged whites feeling they "do good" by helping "underprivileged" (i.e., culturally inferior) African Americans; or African Americans feeling good about themselves because they shield other African Americans from "lazy Latinas."

As with colorblind racism, other forms of oppression can result from adopting and maintaining a moral identity. McMahon's study (1995) of new mothers showed how their embrace of "mother" as a moral identity led them to become invested in reproducing conventional gender inequalities in their family. In the same way, Wall (2001) studied how the experience of motherhood is shaped by moral and cultural constructs about breastfeeding. The author notes that the breastfeeding discourse bombards mothers with messages moralizing pregnancy and giving the fetus personhood. The breast-feeding discourse also values child-centered parenting and individual responsibility. Women are also barraged, Wall notes, with messages on the cost of social programs.

I illustrate how difficult working conditions—low pay, overwhelming pace, too many tasks to complete in a day's work—and structural inequalities present within Care Inc. made health-care work difficult, in particular for the lower-status African American and Latina staffers. These structural inequalities included the training and supervision of Latina staff by the more senior African American staff; the "gatekeeping" positions several of the African American women held that gave them some power over the mostly Latina/o clients; and the lobbying by some African American staff to ban Spanish language from the workplace. I analyze how health-care practitioners—higher-status white staffers, mid-level Latina staffers, lower-status African American staffers, and lower-status Latina staffers—crafted a moral identity by drawing on the cultural resources (Einwohner, Hollander, and Olson 2000; Williams 1995) available to them, taking advantage of constructs that fall along gender, racial, and class, as well as nationalist lines. For example, the higher-status staffers, all but one white, collectively interpreted their difficult conditions at work as evidence that they were "heroic" workers. The mid- and lower-status Latina staffers felt Latina/o clients were especially "needy" and deserving of special protection; guarding over them was a crucial component of their moral identity. However, the moral identity of African American staffers was threatened, as they could not base their moral identities on serving "their people" because most of the clients had become Latinas/os over the years. They elevated their self-esteem by falling back on racist stereotypes of Latinas as lazy, unruly opportunists and as irresponsible parents.

An intersectional lens helps us better understand how these health-care practitioners' moral identity was shaped by their differential locations within race, class, and nationality categories, and how the strategies they devised to craft and maintain their moral identity were shaped by and in turn shaped new ethnic relations and new forms of social membership. I explore how these social dynamics determined not only the lives of the Latina/o immigrants but also the lives of the residents, as newcomers and established residents were thrown together—at work, at school, and in local governments and communities. The ways these health-care providers created a superior self-image reproduced inequalities by dividing lower-status workers, enforcing racial boundaries, and limiting access to health care for patients of the "other" race.

Methods and Perspective

My study was conducted at the (pseudonymous) Care Inc. clinic, a private, not-for-profit community health clinic that provides comprehensive care and education to racially and ethnically diverse clients, now mostly Latinas/os. Using fieldnotes from participant observation and transcripts of in-depth interviews, I analyze how health-care workers reproduced or responded to inequalities of race, class, and gender in their interactions with each other and in their daily work with clients (Schwalbe 2007). I examine these inequalities in an understaffed setting in which health-care providers faced an overload of clients.

Fieldworker Role

Even before the first day of fieldwork (as a researcher and volunteer), I was eager to explore how white US health-care providers, especially those facing difficult working conditions at community clinics, responded to Spanish-speaking immigrants (Williams and Correa 2003). Did the health-care providers share the fear and resentment of some North Carolinians about the influx of Latinas/os (Hyde and Leiter 2000)? How did decreases in health-care services for immigrants (which put more pressure on those services remaining) and an increase in anti-immigrant attitudes by North Carolinians shape health-care workers' conceptions of Latinas/os?

During the more than year and a half of my fieldwork, I felt at ease at the clinic in many ways. I was surrounded mostly by Latinas and Latina/o clients who came for medical care. I felt comfortable with their hearty voices and laughter, their colorful clothes, and their children running around the clinic. Our commonalities—and my relative (middle-class, educated, English proficient) privilege—made it easy for me to feel sympathetic to their plights as poor immigrants. The Latina/o clients were mostly undocumented and spoke little English. Like them, I have brown skin and could understand firsthand what a stigmatizing effect skin color has in the United States.

I also hit it off well with the Latina staff. We often shared our difficulties understanding Southerners' speech, especially when they spoke fast and used slang; we also felt inadequate because of our accents. Latina staffers and I also recalled memories of our youth, especially holidays and the banquets served by our grandmothers and mothers. And we shared a concern for the condition of poor Latina/o clients.

It was much more difficult for me to interact with the African American and white (female) staff at the clinic. Of the forty employees, thirteen were white, fourteen were African American, and twelve were Latina. One employee was Asian American. Because they worked at a community clinic that served mostly Latinas/os, I expected the white and African American staffers to serve as allies to Latinas/os. Given the history of racism in the United States, I thought I might find some discrimination on the part of the white staff toward Latinas/os (staff and clients), and between the white staff and the African American staff, as well as between the white staff and African American clients. That was not the case, however.

I observed hostility between the African American staff and Latina/o staff, between African American staff and Latina/o clients, and occasionally between Latina staff and African American clients. I thought African Americans and Latinas/os would feel solidarity, given their shared racial/ethnic and class interests (Kaufmann 2003; Mindiola, Niemann, and Rodríguez 2002). Initially, I could not understand why the African American staffers seemed to take out their frustration on Latina/o clients and Latina staff, and not on the privileged white staff.

Early in my fieldwork, I took notes about how African American staff treated Latina/o clients dismissively. For example, when I worked alongside the African American receptionist at the clinic, she would hang up the phone and forward a call from a Spanish speaker to me, saying: "Some people call so much, they drive you crazy." She also complained constantly about the noises made by the Latina/o children in the clinic's waiting room.

It was also common for the receptionist and the triage nurse (both African American women) to comment on the Latinas' parenting skills (Latinos [the men] were not usually judged for their parenting abilities): "We would never let our children behave like this." The "we," it seemed, were African American women.

When I translated Spanish for the African American lead nurse, she often asked me why "your people" would do things that were "just not right." She made it clear that she, and by implication other African Americans, would act differently (i.e., by learning to speak English and by not bringing their children to the clinic).

Doing this research heightened my relatively keen awareness of my own "brownness." I regularly asked myself: How does my racial and ethnic identity shape my relationships with the people I am studying? How does it determine who will say what to me, or my understanding of what I see and hear? I knew the early answer to these questions: Profoundly. However, the knowledge produced is not entirely determined by my brown (Latina) racial and ethnic identity. As Mani (1990) wrote, regarding the politics of location (to paraphrase Adrienne Rich [2001]) or the social organization of specific bodies in specific spaces/places, "The relation between experience and knowledge is . . . one not of correspondence, but fraught with history, contingency, and struggle" (26). Every day during my fieldwork, to the best of my capacity, I brought to bear my understanding and awareness of this contingent connection between subjectivity and the production of knowledge. The analysis and story that follows is, as a result, a partial truth mediated by my subjectivity and by my analytical mediation.

I conducted this ethnography as part of my doctoral dissertation, from May 2002 to December 2003, acting as a participant observer and volunteer. In the year and a half I performed fieldwork, I visited the clinic three days a week for five to six hours a day. In my volunteer role, I "floated" through four of the six units. I observed and worked with the staff at the front desk, the Maternity Care Coordination program, the Women, Infants, and Children (WIC) nutrition department, and the clinical unit. The Maternity Care Coordination program provides family planning and contraceptive counseling for all women who come for a free pregnancy test. The maternity care coordinators (MCCs) see all new prenatal clients before their first visit with a clinician, and in this one-hour visit, they provide clients with information about the clinic's services, the WIC nutrition program, and North Carolina's Baby Love program. The WIC program provides a supplemental food package—in the form of vouchers—to pregnant, postpartum (up to six months), and breastfeeding women (up to one year), and infants and children up to their fifth birthday. Recipients must meet financial eligibility (below poverty level) and be at medical or nutritional risk. The clinical or medical unit provides health-care services for children, teens, adults, and seniors, as well as women's health, wellness, and prenatal care. The medical unit also provides physical exams (required for school, employment, sports, nursing homes, etc.), immunizations, flu shots, and laboratory services on-site.

I began my fieldwork after a center manager for the clinic was hired. I committed to work as a volunteer under the supervision of the center manager, where needed, for three days a week for the duration of my study. The center manager and I decided I would begin my fieldwork by observing/working in the reception area. I would then observe/work in referrals, after which I would observe/work in registration and medical records. Following that, I observed/volunteered for the maternity care coordinators, after which I observed/ volunteered for the triage nurse and the WIC program. Finally, I observed the nursing station, the laboratory, and the doctors.

I took notes while in the field (observational/descriptive field-notes). I then typed my notes and took other notes after I returned from the field (expanded/reflective/analytical fieldnotes). I began analyzing the data by writing notes-on-notes (Kleinman and Copp 1993, 60), then analytic memos (Lofland and Lofland 1995). Simultaneously collecting and analyzing the data enabled me to likewise simultaneously test my explanations and modify my interview guide. In my observational fieldnotes, I recorded specific details and facts (Who was there? What happened? What did I notice? What were people wearing? What could I hear? What did I smell?) and recorded approximate transcriptions of conversations and language (e.g., English or Spanish). When people spoke, I wrote down specific words, phrases, and language. As much as possible, I transcribed conversations word for word. I also paid attention to nonverbal cues: How did the people use body language? How did people understand/interpret that body language? (Kleinman and Copp, 62). In my reflective fieldnotes, I noted aspects that I wanted to pay special attention to during upcoming observations; questions arising as possibilities for my final ethnographic project; and/or questions I had about a health-care practitioner or a procedure that I needed to ask an insider about in a future interview.

Most of my data are the recorded detailed fieldnotes of my observations of the daily activities of the health-care workers as they and time permitted. I interviewed twenty-one of the forty employees, including employees who worked at the front desk (center manager, reception, registration, client care coordination [or referrals], billing, and medical records); clinical area (triage nurse, nursing station, laboratory, and doctors); maternity-care coordination program; and WIC nutrition department. Most of these interviews took place outside the clinic, either during interviewees' lunchtime, after work, or on a day off. Three interviews were conducted at the clinic, in an office where no one could hear or interrupt us. Interviews lasted from one to two hours and were transcribed in full.

I ended up interviewing a greater percentage of white higher-status staff (nine of thirteen white staff members) and Latina lower-status staff (eight of twelve Latina staff members) than of African American lower-status staff (five of fourteen African American staff members). These numbers are not a fair representation of the amount of time

I talked to the staff members, however, in particular to the African American lower-status staff. As I worked (volunteered/observed) alongside these staff members, I conducted many informal or mini-interviews. These conversations were extensively recorded in my field-notes, and readers will see evidence of them in the following sections.

The activities of a volunteer were well suited to the job of observer. I hung around without being in the way, listened to and participated in conversations with staff and clients, and watched their daily routines. Asking questions was an expected part of the volunteer role.

I came to know each staff person well. They seemed comfortable talking to me about themselves, other staff, and clients (of all races and ethnicities). I wish I could say it was because of my stellar personality, but instead there are good sociological reasons for this. As a graduate student, I had achieved a higher class status than most of the Latinas and the African American women at the clinic. Thus, for the African American staff, I may have reinforced the impression that the majority of Latinas/os are lesser—after all, I am the exception. I "proved" to the African American staff that Latinas/os could assimilate, speak English well, and so on, if they chose to. As I will show, African American women on staff described Latina staff and clients as "lazy," "bad mothers," and abusers of subsidized health care, in many cases with images that singled out women. Though these stereotypes were not of their own making, African Americans drew on them to create a moral identity as health-care practitioners and claim status over the new and threatening "other" group: Latinas/os. As a PhD student, I broke the stereotype, again serving as the "exception to the rule."

The Latina staff also gave me "extra points" for not being a snob and for being a committed and hard-working volunteer, despite having achieved a higher class status than most Latinas. Similarly, the white staff frequently praised me for being hard working, for never saying "no" when asked to do something or help someone, and for getting along with everyone.

Perspective

This study is grounded in the symbolic interactionist (or interpretative) perspective in sociology (Blumer 1969; Mead 1934), especially as it applies to the reproduction of inequality (Schwalbe et al. 2000).

I focus on how societal and structural pressures acting on health-care providers shaped their behaviors, as well as on the consequences of their behaviors for their clients, other staff members, and themselves. I also approach this study from a feminist (Bartky 1990; Frye 1983; Kleinman 2007; Tong 1998) perspective and use the methodological approach of grounded theory (Charmaz 2000). Grounded theory is an inductive and deductive process whereby theory emerges from data and is then tested (grounded) against "the real world" (513–14).

Mead's pragmatism provides the basis for symbolic interactionism. For Mead, membership in a group gives rise to a set of shared meanings. The different positions and roles individuals hold in a group create differences in people's meanings and behaviors. Mead also contends that culture and social arrangements guide people's behavior rather than rigidly determine it. People can, through individual or joint action, create new meanings, behaviors, and organizational arrangements. Blumer extended Mead's ideas and spelled out three core premises of symbolic interactionism: "[H]uman beings act toward things on the basis of the meaning of such things. . . . [M]eanings [are] social products . . . creations that are formed in and through the defining activities of people as they interact. . . .[A]nd . . . the use of meanings by a person in his [or her] action involves an interpretative process." (2–5)

Some interactionists focus on how people's joint actions create and sustain interactional patterns of equality or inequality (Fields, Copp, and Kleinman 2006). The "sensitizing theory of generic processes in the reproduction of inequality" of Schwalbe et al. (2000, 443) guides this study by pointing out the four major processes in which inequalities are reproduced: othering, subordinate adaptation, boundary maintenance, and emotion management.

Schwalbe et al. define *othering* as the process by which the people in the powerful group define who belongs to the dominant and subordinate groups. Defensive othering is a process through which one group constructs boundaries between its members and other marginalized groups, while at the same time defining itself as morally superior to these (marginalized) "out-groups." *Subordinate adaptation* refers to the coping strategies used by people in the subordinate group to deal with their lower status, many of which strategies reproduce some inequalities while challenging others. *Boundary maintenance* is a process by which inequalities are preserved between the dominant and subordinate groups by controlling subordinates' access to cultural capital, controlling network access, and controlling the means and threats of violence. The last process, *emotion management*, allows people to deal with their demanding work by performing emotional labor to control both their clients/customers and themselves (422–34). When performing emotional labor, workers manage their emotions and the emotions of others in ways that serve the employer's interests (Hall 1993; Hochschild 1983 and 2003; Leidner 1999; Snow and Anderson 1987).

In examining the experience of maintaining a moral identity as it is co-created in conjunction with race and gender by health-care providers in a community clinic in North Carolina, I describe how, despite the fact that economic forces powerfully constrained the way that these health-care workers could do their work (Care Inc. is a very busy and under-resourced clinic that made health-care work stressful), these practitioners lacked a class and race analysis that would have enabled them to comprehend their predicaments. I also show how structural conditions—for example, the training and supervision of Latina staff by the more senior African American staff and the "gatekeeping" positions several of the African American women held that gave them some power over the mostly Latina/o clients—shaped their work and their sense of doing good for the most vulnerable and underserved population of North Carolina. Although African American, white, and Latina staffers occasionally understood the lack of health-care services and their working conditions in terms of the consequences of racism and poverty, they more often than not spoke of the consequences for their patients and co-workers of individual choices, dysfunctional families, lack of education, and lack of English proficiency.

I was guided by Bettie's (2003) analytical frame and perspective, with which she theorizes how race and class are articulated and experienced within racial *and* class groups (as opposed to assuming that all white, working-class girls feel the same way about their class identity), and with which she theorizes how expressions of gender identity are intersected by particular "ethnic strategies" by the Mexican American, working-class, and middle-class girls for whom success at school is often understood as "acting white." By extension, I draw attention to the structure of the community clinic, its formal and informal work procedures, and both the gender and racial/ethnic identities of its workers, to analyze the role of the workplace in the creation of a moral identity and in the reproduction of inequality.

Bettie analyzes the various identity performances of working-class and middle-class Mexican American and white students as they negotiate their senior year in a California public high school. Bettie contends that unequal distribution of class-based cultural capital naturalizes social inequality between the different social and racial groupings at the school (e.g., "las chicas," "hicks," and "preps"). Bettie shows how the "preps"—whose wealth, cultural capital, and school-sanctioned performances of white, middle-class femininity facilitated and supported their advancement to college and careers—were blind to their own advantages and oblivious to the class injuries caused by their comfortable fit with social expectations. White, working-class "smokers" and "skaters," and Mexican American "cholas" and "chicas," resented the ease of the preps' academic and social successes and felt disparaged by the preps' and school authorities' disdain. Non-preps thus felt excluded by school organizations and ceremonies. Bettie analyzes how these feelings of resentment by white working-class and Mexican American students never coalesced into politicized class identities. Instead, these non-prep students blamed themselves and their families for their academic failure and dismal prospects beyond high school, griped about the preps' snobbishness, and asserted their difference through style and rejection of school norms. Bettie highlights how these high school seniors actively participated in the creation of their own identity and their defiant outsider status. White working-class "smokers" and "skaters," and Mexican American "cholas" and "chicas," exercised agency in their choices to skip class, wear darker or lighter lipstick or tighter or looser clothing, pay attention in class or not, visit a business college program or apply to a four-year college. Bettie effectively demonstrates how these high school girls actively shape their social worlds as they perform race/class/gender identities that are created relationally. She contends that "class is a relational identity; awareness of class difference is dependent upon the class and race geography of the environment in which one lives and moves." (144)

As with Bettie, I highlight in the following analysis how health-care providers at a community clinic in North Carolina group themselves according to ethnic/racial origins and use gendered and racialized norms to define "worthy" patients as well as "good" and "moral" workers. The definitions of worthy patients and moral workers are oppositional and relational. The ways health-care providers understand and articulate who are worthy patients and who are moral workers are defined by each racial/ethnic health-care provider group and in opposition to one another. I demonstrate how the different providers draw on local and semiautonomous sources of meaning to create and maintain their moral identity. As a result, I show how "moral identity" is always constructed through race/ethnicity, nationality, class, and gender.

NOTE: The critical feminist analysis that follows is not meant as a critique of individual people or groups of people in the clinic, but as an analysis of patterns of inequality demonstrated to develop when any people or group of people—even those with the best of intentions—are subjected to pressure within specific social and relational structures. Many people provided invaluable feedback for this work, but I take sole responsibility for the views expressed here.

2

"El Nuevo South"

The Case of North Carolina and the Community Health Center Program

La Nueva Carolina del Norte

NEWCOMERS FROM MEXICO and other Latin American countries have long served as flexible, low-wage agricultural labor in Florida and California. Recently, these newcomers have been incorporated into expanding low-wage industries, like poultry production and other food processing, in rural areas of North Carolina and Georgia (Cravey 1997), as well as into the rapidly increasing service and construction sectors in "Sun Belt" cities like Atlanta and Durham, North Carolina (Johnson, Johnson-Webb, and Farrell 1999). In these areas the arrival of new immigrants complicates binary understandings of racial categories as "black" and "white," giving rise to complex shifts in cultural understandings of what it means to belong to a community in the new "transnational South."

Newcomers to North Carolina, mostly from Mexico, have been described as

> one of the mainstays of the agricultural workforce, and they are disproportionately employed in hazardous industries, such as construction, or in low-paying jobs. . . . Almost two-thirds of North Carolina Latinos (64.2 percent) are foreign-born, with almost half reporting that they do not speak English very well. Over half of the Latinos in the state are noncitizens (58.3 percent).

. . . Most North Carolina Latinos are recent immigrants from
Mexico (65.1 percent). (Silberman et al. 2003, 113)

According to Kasarda and Johnson's report for the Kenan Institute
(2006), Latina/o fiscal impact on North Carolina's budget totaled an
estimated $817 million in 2004, which included the costs of educa-
tion, health services, and corrections. But those costs were balanced
to a large degree, according to this report, by direct and indirect tax
contributions of $756 million, resulting in a net cost to the state
budget of $61 million—approximately $102 per Latina/o resident.
Meanwhile, despite the perception among North Carolinians that
these newcomers are taking away residents' jobs and "their" (very
limited) social and medical services, Latina/o immigrants' important
economic contribution, through purchases, taxes, labor, and contributions to Social Security and Medicare (from which they will never
receive benefits), has been shown to surpass their estimated cost to
the state budget. As for the African American population in North
Carolina, Kasarda and Johnson estimated that the fiscal impact of
African Americans on the state budget totaled $4.5 billion in 2004,
which included the costs of education, health services, and corrections. Those costs were balanced, according to this report, to a large
degree by direct and indirect tax contributions of $3.8 billion, result-
ing in a net cost to the state budget of $759 million—approximately
$420 per African American resident.

Despite the perception among North Carolinians that these newcomers do not pay taxes, all newcomers pay sales taxes when they pur-
chase goods and pay property taxes if they own property. Many newcomers also pay income taxes. Newcomers who are legally employed
have wages withheld for tax purposes. In addition, between one-half
and three-quarters of unauthorized immigrants are estimated to pay
federal and state income taxes, Social Security taxes, and Medicare
taxes (Economic Report of the President 2005), as they use false
Social Security numbers to work "on the books" and, as a result, pay
payroll taxes when their wages are withheld. A study by the Center for
Immigration Studies estimated that in 2002 these unauthorized immigrants contributed more than $7 billion in taxes to Social Security and
Medicare, federal programs from which they cannot receive benefits
(Camarota 2004). As noted above, a Kenan Institute study found that

Hispanic residents in North Carolina—US–born citizens, authorized immigrants, and unauthorized immigrants—paid an estimated $756 million in state and local taxes in 2004 (Kasarda and Johnson 2006).

Between 1995 and 2005, Latina/o newcomers contributed more than $9 billion to North Carolina's economy, filling one in three new jobs created in North Carolina, with significant concentrations in the construction industry (29 percent of the labor force) (Kasarda and Johnson 2006). Latinas/os were also employed in the forestry and agricultural industries in rural areas, as well as in the traditional (and declining) North Carolina manufacturing industries: meat processing, textiles, and household furniture (Acury et al. 1999). Within these industries, the Latina/o labor force is primarily concentrated in operative, labor, and service jobs (Skaggs, Tomaskovic-Devey, and Leiter 2000). The Latina labor force is overrepresented in the service industry. Many Latinas are hired as maids, janitors, meat-processing workers, cashiers, nannies, cooks, or agricultural workers (Karjanen 2008; Kasarda and Johnson 2006, 17).

Newcomers mow lawns, paint homes, watch children, and cook food, all for bottom-tier wages. In doing so, newcomers provide residents with affordable services. However, because many newcomers work for below-market wages, North Carolina private-sector wages have gone down. According to Kasarda and Johnson (2006), private-sector payrolls diminished by $1.9 billion annually (1995–2005). Without Latina/o labor, the state's total private sector wage bill would be $1.9 billion higher (35). The lower wages have affected established residents, both white and African American. However, newcomers are more likely to work alongside African Americans, as African Americans are concentrated mainly in blue-collar occupations such as trucking, freight handling, janitorial and maid service, and landscaping. Both groups are also employed in administrative/secretarial support and other white-collar (mainly direct-service) occupations in the health-care, retail, and education sectors of the North Carolina economy (Kasarda and Johnson 2007, 15).

Race and the Changing Workplace

Waldinger and Lichter (2003), who analyze the Los Angeles low-wage labor market, found that native-born African American workers, according to their employers in printing services, department stores, hospitals, hotels, restaurants, and furniture manufacturing, have higher expectations for wages and working conditions; native-born workers, it appears, are at a disadvantage compared to immigrant workers because they have both the expectation of better conditions and the language to express their demands. As a result, immigrant workers are preferred to US workers by some employers, as immigrants are "here to work" and do not talk back or have "negative attitudes," as their frame of reference is the country they left behind. Thus, immigrant workers who lack English, schooling, and familiarity with US culture are preferred to US workers by some employers because of their "personal qualifications—friendliness, enthusiasm, and smiling subservience" (220). Waldinger and Lichter contend that employers seek workers who they anticipate will give them the least trouble in terms of attitude, and therefore other ethnic groups are preferred by some employers over African American workers. Some employers feel that African American workers shun jobs that are perceived by most native-born workers as being beneath them. Immigrant workers, on the other hand, are often desperate for work and are much more willing to work for less money and at demanding types of employment that US workers would refuse.

Similarly, Broadway, Stull, and Podraza (1994) describe how the search for immigrant labor became imperative for the meatpacking plants' management (and has continued to the present) as a consequence of the high turnover in the plants due to the exhausting and dangerous working conditions. These bad conditions give the immigrants their opening—constant turnover makes for vacancies, and the companies are always on the lookout for a pliable, cheap labor force—while also limiting the prospects for upward movement. Broadway et al. describe both the consequences of the restructuring of the US economy as well as the impact of immigration on the workplace in Garden City, Kansas, a town of approximately 18,000 in 1980, which increased its industrial employment by 55 percent in the subsequent eight years, mainly through Southeast Asian and Mexican migrants. The meatpacking industry, as a result, has acquired a diverse labor force, with Southeast Asian refugees, Mexicans, and other Latinos working alongside long-term white residents. The authors conclude that relations among the different ethnic groups are often amicable at work, but that deep divisions exist nonetheless, built on residential segregation and an immigrant pecking order in which Southeast Asians obtain the worst jobs, Mexican and other Latino immigrants obtain better ones, and non-Hispanic whites disproportionately dominate the upper tiers of management.

Although for the most part immigrant workers complain little about hours and conditions, and come to the factory and other workplaces every day with a tremendous work ethic, Fink (2003) describes how Maya migrants from Guatemala working in a chicken-processing plant in Morganton, North Carolina, quickly organized and made an alliance with older Mexican workers. As in Los Angeles and Garden City, Kansas, unpleasant work conditions made it increasingly difficult for poultry companies to attract US-born workers, and as a result, Guatemalans, Salvadorans, Mexicans, and other foreign workers immigrated and settled in towns throughout poultry-producing states. Fink contends that the turmoil in modern-day Guatemala prepared these Maya workers for unpleasant bosses and working conditions, as well as for the perils of protest.

Waldinger and Lichter, in their 2003 study of the Los Angeles low-wage labor market, contend that immigrants in the past were encouraged to learn some English in order to interact with their English-speaking supervisors at work. English proficiency, in the past, was the key to jobs and higher wages. Today, immigrants who work within ethnic enclaves do not feel the economic pressure to learn English. Therefore, Waldinger and Lichter conclude that unless the United States makes a concerted effort to foster immigrant integration, the long-term effect is continued racial and ethnic conflict between native-born and recent-immigrant members of the lower classes, and the continued downward spiral of the African American community. Similarly, Broadway et al. (1994) warn of a continued downward spiral for immigrant communities, as immigrant workers enter the low-wage labor market and the economy at the very bottom, during a time when worker protections have been weakened and unions are in disarray.

Immigration and Racial Tensions

In North Carolina, news reports call attention to the existence of prejudices against Latinas/os by whites and by African Americans who believe North Carolina and the United States in general are becoming "a brown planet," as "most Mexicanos don't practice birth control [and] they have litters of babies" (Browder 2006; Chavez 2001). However, in North Carolina, as nationally, African Americans' prejudices against newcomers seem to be more pronounced than those of whites. In California, nearly 50 percent of African Americans supported Proposition 187 (a 1994 voter-initiated policy designed to deny public services to undocumented immigrants). A 2006 Pew Research Center survey of 2,000 adults nationwide found that more African Americans (33 percent) saw immigrants as taking away jobs from US citizens than did either whites (25 percent) or Latinas/os (9 percent). Of those African Americans surveyed, 54 percent said that undocumented immigrants should not be eligible for social services provided by state or local governments, and 21 percent said that the children of undocumented immigrants should not be allowed to attend public schools. The same survey found that 75 percent of African Americans said that increased immigration has led to difficulties in finding a job, and 22 percent of African Americans responded that they or a relative had lost a job to an immigrant (2006).

In writing about the Minutemen, a volunteer organization that functions as a paramilitary guard at borders, airports, and other points of entry for immigrants to the United States, Hutchinson (2006a) notes:

> The Minutemen's pitch to Blacks is a shrewd, cynical ploy to capitalize on the split among Blacks over illegal immigration. . . . An April Field Poll in California found that Blacks, by a bigger percentage than whites and even American-born Latinos, back liberal immigration reform. But many Blacks express views that are wildly at odds with . . . the polls. Black callers have singed the phone lines at Black radio talk shows with anti-immigrant tirades. They bombard Black newspapers with letters blasting illegal immigrants. They complain that Latinos are hostile, even racist, toward Blacks.

As these polls and opinions demonstrate, the unprecedented Latina/o immigration to North Carolina has been accompanied by racial tensions. When North Carolinians—African American and white—were asked in 1996 about the increase of the Latina/o population in North Carolina (from 1.2 percent of the total in 1990 to almost 3 percent in 2000), 40 percent of respondents said they were unhappy about it and that growth was a problem. When asked about how they would feel if Latinas/os moved into their neighborhoods, about 67 percent said they would not like it, and more than 90 percent said they would dislike having Hispanics as neighbors (Hyde and Leiter 2000).

A major oral history initiative launched by the Southern Oral History Program at the University of North Carolina–Chapel Hill has documented these racial tensions and struggles among "old-timers" and their "new" neighbors in various communities in North Carolina. One project focused on the impact of Latina/o immigration in Durham. Jill Hemming, Alicia J. Rouverol, and Angela Hornsby (2001) recorded "life . . . before the arrival of Latino newcomers, the experience of Latino immigrants, and the challenges that African Americans, Latinos, and whites have faced as they find strategies to live in shared spaces" (10).

The Latina/o immigrant population settling in North Carolina has been unprecedented, and, for many old-time residents, inexplicable, the authors observed. As one African American old-timer said: "I was curious to know if there's something that's going on in Durham that I don't know about that's attracting all the Latino population" (29). The influx of Latinas/os has also been associated with danger and distrust. As another African American resident explained: "You're talking about a whole different culture that you want me to trust myself with. No, no, no, no. That's taking me out of my comfort zone first of all, and then you are asking me to do something I don't understand because I don't speak Spanish" (29–30).

Another African American old-timer expressed strong and negative feelings about the changes in his neighborhood due to the "newcomers": "Well, when I started seeing the Hispanics moving in, I felt that they were invading on my turf, on my playground. It was no longer our place. . . . [In] '89, that's when I started to see that the community was changing. And along in that time, too, crime was building. The community that I knew and loved and grew up in and felt safe in had already changed. So with the Hispanics moving in, that didn't help any" (27–29).

Many respondents also viewed Latinas/os as criminals, and as taking advantage of welfare programs and jobs at the expense of US citizens, especially African Americans. As an African American old-timer said: "I've heard horror stories how if you want to get some cheap labor you go get a Mexican. I'm talking about contractors coming in here paying Hispanics less than what they could pay an African American because they knew that they could pay them less. Maybe because they were illegal immigrants or didn't know any better. So in turn, it was cutting out the African American from doing the only job he could do" (31).

The Latinas/os interviewed were aware of others' prejudices toward them. One of the new residents said: "Here, they think poorly of us. The same thing happens even at work: They always prefer people that are from here rather than people that are not from here, like us" (34).

Although some Latinas/os complained about white racism, for many the bigger problem seemed to be conflicts with African Americans. As a Latina respondent said to the researchers, "I don't like the Black people; sometimes they look at us saying: 'You are nothing'" (34–35).

Warranted or not, racial tensions between African Americans and Latinas/os exist in American communities and institutions (Hutchinson 2006b, 2007; Summers 2006); and North Carolina's Research Triangle, as well as Care Inc., were no exception. Larger social and economic forces such as globalization (e.g., jobs moving overseas), the declining manufacturing sector, and shrinking state provisions for welfare and social services are partly to blame for the erosion of gains within the African American community (Darity and Myers 1998), but these appear distant and abstract compared to actors in their immediate environment. Local community members are more likely to highlight firsthand accounts of Latinas/os moving into their neighborhoods and using community resources (Massey 2008; Pew Hispanic Center 2007; Santa Ana 2002).

Tensions among African Americans and Latinas/os are not exclusive to North Carolina (Gay 2006; Lambert and Taylor 1990; McClain et al. 2006). For example, Mindiola, Niemann, and Rodriguez (2002) show how both African Americans and Latinas/os in the Houston metropolitan area accept and reinforce the most extreme and harmful stereotypes held by whites. The negativity in most of the stereotypes held by the African American and brown respondents tended to focus on competition for jobs, the availability of needed but limited social services, the quality of education in their neighborhoods, and access to the political power structure in the city of Houston. For many of the African American respondents, in particular women, the spread of the Spanish language was a particularly troublesome issue, and as a consequence they expressed particular disdain for the use of Spanish in public places of business, those areas in which cross-community relations most frequently occur. On the other hand, Latinas/os, both foreign-born and US-born, expressed a view of African Americans as being a favored community and as the perennial beneficiaries of governmental programs for minorities, in particular since the civil rights movement. As a result, the authors contend, both groups are susceptible to divide-and-conquer tactics, which have kept whites in power for decades.

By focusing on Care Inc., a work site and a location where Latina/o newcomers and residents—African Americans and whites—frequently interact, I provide a glimpse into the integration process of Latina/o newcomers in "el Nuevo South" (Fink 2003). First analyzing the transformations in North Carolina from the viewpoint of both resident and newcomer health-care practitioners—who have struggled with the consequences of migration on their everyday lives, families, and communities—I then explore the North Carolina community transformation from the perspectives of both recent Mexican immigrants to North Carolina and the established resident health-care practitioners, and how this transformation has shaped the meaning of health-care work. Similarly, I examine how these definitions of health-care work shape the relationships between established resident health-care practitioners and newcomer Latina practitioners and, finally, how race plays a role in the development of a moral identity.

The Community Health Center Program

Because it is right . . . I submit . . . the Economic Opportunity Act of 1964. The Act . . . charts a new course. It strikes at the causes, not just the consequences of poverty. It can be a milestone in our . . . search for a better life for our people. . . . It will give almost

half a million underprivileged young Americans the opportunity
to develop skills, continue education, and find useful work. It will
give every American community the opportunity to develop a comprehensive plan to fight its own poverty—and help them to carry
out their plans. It will give dedicated Americans the opportunity
to enlist as volunteers in the war against poverty. It will give many
workers and farmers the opportunity to break through particular
barriers which bar their escape from poverty. . . . What you are being
asked to consider is not a simple or an easy program. But poverty
is not a simple or an easy enemy. It cannot be driven from the land
by a single attack on a single front. Were this so we would have
conquered poverty long ago. Nor can it be conquered by government alone. . . . Today, for the first time in our history, we have the
power to strike away the barriers to full participation in our society.
Having the power, we have the duty.

—*Proposal for "A Nationwide War on the Sources of Poverty,"*
Lyndon B. Johnson's Special Message to Congress, March 16, 1964

Neighborhood health centers, also known as community health centers, were a result of Democratic president Johnson's "War on Poverty." In the early 1960s, the US federal government took on the
responsibility of providing health-care services and increasing access to
health care for the elderly and the poor. Both Medicare and Medicaid
were enacted into law in 1964, designed to increase access to health
care for the elderly and the poor by having the government pay providers and hospitals for medical services (Sardell 1988).

In 1965 the US Office of Economic Opportunity gave grants to
community groups—health departments, community organizations,
hospitals, and medical schools—to set up and administer health centers in poor neighborhoods. The idea was that these health centers
would "provide high-quality health care to low-income populations
lacking access to such care and, at the same time, serve as a model
for the reorganization of health-care services for the entire US population" (Sardell, 4). This radical health-services innovation was a
response to the "discovery of poverty . . . , a fear of urban unrest . . . ,
and a broader concern for the needs of the urban poor, primarily
minorities" (6). The survival of the health-center program was in
question when Presidents Richard Nixon and Gerald Ford, both
Republicans, took office. Nixon, for example, planned on reducing

Johnson's social programs and placing health initiatives in the private sector. Ford, on the other hand, vetoed the Special Health Revenue Sharing Act of 1975, which would have established the community health-center program as a separate categorical grant program. The legislation was enacted after Congress overrode his veto (109).

The health-center program survived and was later expanded by Democratic President Jimmy Carter. By 1980, approximately 880 community centers existed and were providing medical health services to approximately six million people (President's Commission 1983, 131). In 1995, 822 health centers operated in the United States and served almost nine million patients (NACHC 1996). In 2001, 845 health centers were serving almost 12 million clients in the United States (Rosenbaum and Shin 2003, 3); slightly more than half of them (51 percent) operated in rural communities (2).

In the United States, the poor and elderly are disproportionately female, and the poor are also disproportionately people of color. This is reflected in the clientele of community health centers like Care Inc. In 2001, 59 percent of all health-center patients were female and 64 percent were members of racial or ethnic minority groups. Thirty-five percent were Hispanic and 25 percent were African American (Rosenbaum and Shin 2003, 6).

Some community health centers emerged from working-class and anti-racist social movements. Common goals forged close ties between members of the civil rights movement and members of the community health-center movement. The health needs of African American communities, particularly in the South, often led the African American community and people involved in the civil rights movement to establish health centers (Couto 1991; Kiefer 2000). The community clinic I studied was established by prominent members of the African American community in North Carolina to help meet the health-care needs of African American people.

Today, people of color, immigrants, the elderly, and the poor still have difficulty accessing quality health care. As Bayne-Smith, Graham, and Guttmacher (2005) explain: "Historically, race in the United States has served as the basis for denial of social justice and access to resources and critical services. However, it is now of serious concern that in the opening decade of the twenty-first century, the burden of health disparities in the nation continues to fall primarily on the poor, a disproportionate number of whom are members of racial and ethnic populations" (25).

According to recent estimates, there are more than 10 million undocumented immigrants living in the United States (Passel and Suro 2005). Because undocumented immigrants are more likely to lack private insurance and have the lowest rates of public insurance, they are more likely than citizens to rely on community clinics for health services (Staiti, Hurley, and Katz 2006, 1). The demand on community health centers by immigrants (undocumented or not) varies by state (and city). The states of California and New Jersey and the cities of Miami and Phoenix have had to respond to immigrants' demands for health services for many years. Other states have few year-round immigrant residents. States such as North Carolina and Arkansas are only recently confronting a large influx of immigrants from Latin America; they are coping with new, sudden, and urgent problems (Staiti, Hurley, and Katz 2006):

> [U]ndocumented immigrants can typically access primary care through safety-net providers, but providers report more difficulty referring undocumented immigrants for specialty care. In several communities, waiting times to see specialists in safety-net hospitals have reportedly increased, with waiting times the longest for the uninsured. Other problem areas mentioned include the provision of chronic care treatment, mental-health care, and obtaining affordable prescription drugs, because program rules often impede services for undocumented patients. (2)

The same study reported that immigrants trying to access health care face language and cultural barriers as well as political backlash in the form of anti-immigrant initiatives attempting to limit social services (3).

Community health centers have become a major source of health care for the poor (Kiefer 2000). According to a report by the Commonwealth Fund (Collins et al. 2002), 20 percent of Latinas/os in the United States regularly go to a community health center for medical care. Community health clinics are also a significant source of health care to the non-Latino poor: 10 percent of African Americans, 8 percent of Asian Americans, and 7 percent of non-Latino whites use health centers as their usual source of care in the United States (Collins et al. 2002). This same survey found that 28 percent of Latinas/os, 24 percent of Asian Americans, 22 percent of African Americans, and 15 percent of non-Latino whites feel they have "very little choice" or "no choice" in where they obtain health care, and rely either on area community health centers or hospital emergency rooms. About 14 percent of Latinas/os fall back on emergency rooms—or have no source of care—compared with 6 percent of non-Latino whites, 8 percent of Asian Americans, and 13 percent of African Americans.

The most costly care provided is at hospital emergency rooms (Agency for Healthcare Research and Quality 2008). Uninsured North Carolinians who rely on hospital emergency rooms for health care ended up costing the state and hospitals approximately $1.4 billion for uncompensated care in 2005, according to research compiled by Families USA, a national consumer advocacy group (Easterbrook and Fisher 2006). According to the North Carolina Hospital Association, there are 1.3 million North Carolinians who have no health insurance, and approximately a third of them are undocumented immigrants. According to the North Carolina Division of Medical Assistance, the state's Medicaid manager, undocumented-immigrant health-care spending by Medicaid (the joint local-state-federal health insurance program for the poor) doubled from $25.8 million in 2000 to $52.8 million in 2005. Still, care for undocumented immigrants absorbs just a small portion of North Carolina's total Medicaid spending: in fiscal year 2005, the cost of care for undocumented immigrants was less than one half of 1 percent of the Medicaid program's total budget of $8.2 billion (Easterbrook and Fisher 2006).

The lack of affordable health insurance and the rising costs of health care are two factors accounting for the substandard quality of and limited access to medical care for the poor (Collins et al. 2002). According to the US Census Bureau Poverty Report (Dalaker 2001), 22.7 percent of African Americans, 21.4 percent of Latinas/os, 10.2 percent of Asians and Pacific Islanders, and 7.8 percent of non-Latino whites live below the poverty level. Latina/o adults have the highest uninsured rates of any racial and ethnic group in the United States. According to findings from the Commonwealth Fund's 2001 health-care quality survey, 46 percent of Latina/o adults did not have health insurance for all or part of 2001. The uninsured rates for non-Latina/o white, Asian American, and African American adults, while lower, are nonetheless high: 20 percent, 21 percent, and 30 percent, respectively.

A Kaiser/Pew survey estimated that nationally, about 35 percent of Latinas/os are uninsured, compared with about 14 percent of non-Latina/o whites. Low-income non-citizens are more than twice as likely to be uninsured as low-income citizens (Kaiser Family Foundation 2003). Of the 11 million low-income non-citizens, 60 percent had no health insurance in 2001 and only 13 percent received Medicaid. In contrast, about 28 percent of low-income citizens were uninsured and about 30 percent had Medicaid (Fiscella et al. 2000, 2002).

For most community clinics, public funding is vital. Community health centers receive funding from Medicaid and Medicare, from state and local funds for indigent care, and from Public Service Act grants for health centers, migrant workers, and the homeless. The health centers also depend on payments from health insurance companies and direct payment from patients (Kiefer 2000, 147).

Community health centers vary by mission, size, and budget, but most of them are non-profit organizations with boards of directors who have financial and policy oversight (see fig. 1; Bayne-Smith, Graham, and Guttmacher 2005, 41). The day-to-day operation of the organization falls to the executive director, who reports to the board of directors and trustees. The executive director is counseled on how to run the health center by its managerial staff, which might include the center manager, the fiscal manager, the director of personnel, the unit directors, and the accountants. Direct services to clients are provided by the clerical support staff—receptionists and patient-care coordinators—and the health-care providers, comprising doctors, nurses, and medical assistants (Bayne-Smith, Graham, and Guttmacher 2005, 43).

We next examine the community clinic where these newcomers and established residents work and interact, followed by a description of some of the threats to the moral identities constructed by the health-care practitioners; finally, we explore how moral-identity construction is a dynamic process that evolves in relation to the pressures of immigration and of the social and cultural contexts in which the resident and newcomer health-care practitioners are working and

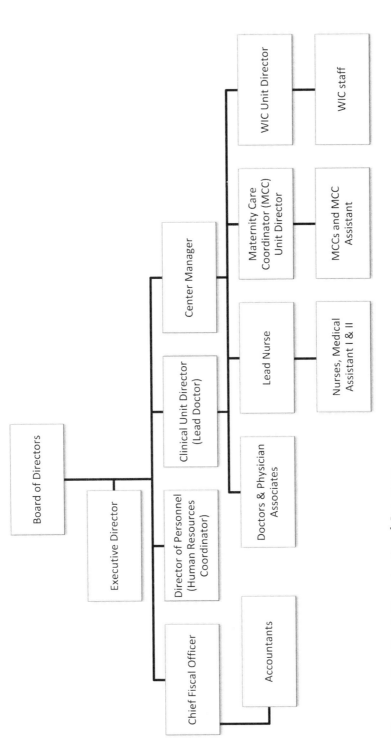

Figure 1. Care Inc.'s Organizational Structure

forging their identities. This study concludes with an examination of evidence that these health-care providers crafted a superior self-image, reproducing inequalities by dividing lower-status workers, enforcing racial boundaries, and limiting access to health care to patients of the "other" race.

The Health-Care Program at Care Inc.:
Serving the Underserved of North Carolina

Care Inc. provides health services to low-income people who otherwise receive inadequate health care and whose access to health services is restricted, especially by their lack of health insurance. As a community clinic, Care Inc. provides health services to people in need who reside in the town and surrounding areas. The town where Care Inc. is located has evolved from a small, relatively rural, turn-of-the-century village, sustained, through the 1940s, by tobacco and textile concerns to, by 2008, a thriving municipality with approximately 55,000 residents and an economy driven by the food processing, technology, and pharmaceutical industries (US Census Data 2008). The demand for health services at this clinic exceeds the center's capacity; many new clients wait three to six months for an appointment. This is not surprising, because 16.5 percent or 1.3 million residents of North Carolina lack health insurance (North Carolina Institute of Medicine 2006).

Care Inc. is a partially federally funded not-for-profit clinic open to the public Monday through Friday, which provides health-care services and education to more than 5,500 clients a year. Sixty-six percent of Care Inc.'s clients are female. Fifty-seven percent are Latinas/os, 17 percent are white, 16 percent are African American, 1 percent are American Indian, and 1 percent are Asian.

The clinic offers "comprehensive" services, including primary and preventive care for children, teens, adults, and older people; physical exams; and laboratory services and flu shots. The clinic also provides reproductive-health services: family planning, free pregnancy testing and counseling, childbirth classes, maternity care coordinators, maternal outreach, certification for the Baby Love program for prenatal care, and gynecological services (including Pap smears). The goal of the Baby Love program, which began in 1987, is to reduce North Carolina's high infant-mortality rate by improving access to health care for low-income pregnant women and children. Through the program, women receive care from the beginning of pregnancy through the postpartum period. Nurses and maternity care coordinators (MCCs) help women obtain medical care and social services (i.e., transportation, housing, job training, and day care). In addition, Maternal Outreach Workers—specially trained home visitors—work with at-risk families to encourage healthy behaviors and ensure that they are linked with community resources. Other services include childbirth and parenting classes, in-home skilled nursing care for high-risk pregnancies, nutrition and psychosocial counseling, and postpartum/newborn home visits (see: http://www.dhhs.state.nc .us/dma/babylove.html). In addition, the clinic offers nutritional services: Women, Infants, and Children Nutrition Program, or WIC; and nutritional and dietary counseling. Clients also have access to a pharmacy and to dental services. (Dental services were terminated in October of 2002 but reopened in 2003.) Although these services are available to any North Carolinian—of any sex or age—women and children were the ones who took advantage of these comprehensive services. As the director of the clinic told me as he showed me around my first day: "The clinic is open to both men and women. Unfortunately, our outreach to men has not been successful. Most of our clients are women and children. Men, usually, do not get preventive health care" (Fieldnotes).

Care Inc. is one of seven clinics run by a corporation I pseudonymously call "Health Services Cooperative" or HSC. When I started my research, this private not-for-profit corporation had been in operation for some thirty years. As a community health provider, HSC receives some funds from the US Department of Health and Human Services. According to its training manual, HSC aims to "assur[e] the availability of affordable primary care services to special populations in the greatest need. Special emphasis is placed on maternity and infant care through a comprehensive perinatal care program . . . [and on] providing high quality of care to all of [their] clients and improving the overall health of [their] communities."

HSC provides primary care services to more than 75,000 clients in six counties. A major emphasis of Care Inc. and five of its sister clinics is "health promotion and disease prevention as well as acute and chronic primary care treatment for families and individuals" (HSC flyer). One of HSC's centers also offers obstetrical services (*Brief History of HSC,* training manual).

The layouts of the individual community clinics vary depending on their buildings, their size, and the services they provide. However, the layout of Care Inc. is similar to that of other community clinics I have visited in North Carolina (see fig. 2). It is a one-story building in a predominantly African American neighborhood. Just inside the clinic doors, several rooms surround a waiting room. To the left, clients can find the dental unit and the pharmacy. To the right are the registration office (now separated from the waiting room by a glass window) and the reception area. Behind the reception area, small rooms house the patient-care coordinator, the billing unit, and the medical records unit. At the end of the hall to the right is another waiting area; here clients wait to see the triage nurse or the doctors. Large glass windows separate the clinic unit from the waiting clients, allowing the latter to see the medical assistants, nurses, and clinicians at work. A hall on the left leads clients past the pharmacy to the Women, Infants, and Children program (WIC) and maternity-care coordination "units," as clinic staff call them. Clients of these units wait in another small waiting area with a glass window. Given the set-up of the clinic, the lower-status staff members—African Americans and Latinas—are in direct contact with the clients, while the white higher-status staff members have more physical separation from clients.

From its inception in the early 1970s, Care Inc. has mainly served the poor. In the mid-1970s, Care Inc.'s clientele was predominantly African American; clients today are primarily Latinas/os. The changing demographics at the clinic reflect the fact that North Carolina has one of the highest rates of Latina/o immigration in the United States (Peacock, Watson, and Matthews 2005, 206). Since 1990 some Southern states, including North Carolina, have become common destinations for Latina/o immigrants. According to the Pew Hispanic Center, in 2004 an estimated 600,000 Latinas/os made North Carolina their home; 70 percent were from Mexico. Some estimate that between 50 and 80 percent of newcomers are undocumented, an estimated 316,000 to 395,000 people (Pew Hispanic

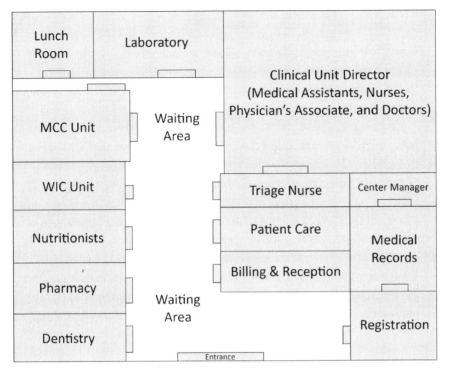

Figure 2. Care Inc.'s Layout

Center 2005). Although most of the clients seen at Care Inc. during my time there were recent migrants from Mexico (65 percent to 70 percent in triage and 95 percent in prenatal care, according to the providers and my own observations), the term Latina/o is employed throughout this book, because a client's actual country of birth was not officially recorded.

According to the US Census Bureau, North Carolina's Latina/o population grew 394 percent from 1990 to 2000; it now accounts for 4.7 percent of the state's population. For the United States as a whole, the growth in the Latina/o population during this same decade was only 60 percent. As the population of newcomers grew, North Carolina health-care providers struggled to meet their needs: "[There are] several health issues facing Latinos in the state, including the current health status of this population; their different health-care expectations; language difficulties; lack of health literacy; financial barriers due to lack of health insurance; inadequate state resources to address the health, behavioral health and dental needs of the growing but largely uninsured Latino population; barriers facing the migrant population; and inadequate data to monitor the Latino population's health status and access to care and services" (Silberman et al. 2003, 113–114).

Care Inc. charged clients for services based on their ability to pay. For a client to be considered for a low fee, as determined by federal guidelines, the client had to provide the clinic with: (1) proof of address; (2) proof of household income; and (3) an insurance card, if she or he had it. Proof of address could be either an envelope or a copy of a bill from the telephone company, electric company, or a copy of a lease, rental agreement, etc. To provide proof of household income, all members of a household had to supply proof of income: a wife had to document her income and that of her husband; people living together and sharing income, even if not related, had to supply proof of income for each individual. A client also presented all insurance cards, whether the insurance was private or public. If clients' household income was at or below the poverty line (determined by the federal government), they were charged scale fee "A" and did not have to pay for medical care; clients whose household income level was at least twice the poverty level were charged scale fee "E," and they paid 100 percent of the cost of the services rendered.

Care Inc. charged a sliding fee because, as asserted on the HSC website: "[M]any people in the areas our clinics serve are in 'underserved areas,' meaning there is not easy accessibility to medical care, or there may not be accessibility to affordable medical care. Our goal, our mission, is to provide quality medical care for all people."

This system increases accessibility (and therefore demand), yet it reduces the resources available to the clinic to meet that demand by underfunding, thereby creating understaffing. It is in this context of underfunding, understaffing, and resultant overwork that the staff at Care Inc. created their moral identity.

Approximately forty employees worked at Care Inc. during my fieldwork. There was turnover: some workers moved to other clinics; staff members from other HSC clinics came to work at Care Inc.; others quit or were put on notice by the center manager; some new staff members were hired. Care Inc. was a very busy and under-resourced place. The forty employees worked in one of six different units, but some of the staff frequently had to work in several different units because of patient demand. I observed staff from the reception area doing registration, billing, client-care coordination, and medical records in one workday. This multitasking was expected, and the training manual describes this as the "team philosophy." Though promoted as "teamwork," my observation showed this multitasking was also stressful and could interrupt or abbreviate the training of a worker in his or her specialty.

Of the forty employees, thirteen were white, fourteen were African American, and twelve were Latina (six were born in Mexico, two in Puerto Rico, two in Venezuela, one in El Salvador, and one in Colombia); one employee was Asian American. Most employees were between 30 and 50 years old. Ninety-five percent of the employees were women; only four men worked at the clinic during my field-work: a white doctor; an African American WIC administrator; a receptionist from Puerto Rico (for less than ten months); and a Mexican medical assistant (for just one month). Only the white doctor and the African American WIC administrator worked at Care Inc. during the entire time I did fieldwork. Eduardo (all names are pseudonyms), the twenty-four-year-old Puerto Rican receptionist, had been in Fort Bragg, North Carolina, for three years and planned to go to school to study engineering, using the GI bill. He often arrived to work several hours late and once missed a day of work because he had to move all his furniture to his cousin's home after being evicted for not paying rent for four months. One day he called saying he had to leave town after a fight with the father of his girlfriend's son, for which he needed five stitches on his right eyebrow. His inability to be punctual and his abrupt departure contributed to the stressful work conditions at Care Inc. Guillermo, a Mexican man in his late 40s, was hired as a medical assistant (I), although he had been trained and had practiced as a medical doctor in Mexico. He spoke English and worked for only a month at Care Inc.

The overwhelming presence of female staff at this community clinic is explained, in part, by gender segregation in the health-care labor force throughout the United States (Butter et al. 1985). Female physicians tend to specialize in public health, pediatrics, and psychiatry, while male physicians tend to specialize in fields such as surgery and pathology. As Butter et al. explain, "Historically women physicians have had a propensity to cluster in salaried employment and in bureaucratic work settings in contrast to the highly autonomous, self-employed practice mode of their male peers." (25) Community clinics like Care Inc., then, are often staffed largely by women and, because there are usually more lower-status jobs than higher-status jobs in such clinics, the majority of staff members are likely to be women of color (27).

The health field is also racially segregated. People of color make up the majority of lower-status health-care providers, while the more prestigious and better-paying sector is dominated by whites (34). The intersection of racial and gender segregation results in a staff profile like that of Care Inc. and of most community clinics. Nurses, social workers, health educators, and medical assistants are predominantly women; white women hold the higher-paying of these jobs and women of color fill the positions at the lower-paying level (36).

At Care Inc., the racial composition of the staff seemed relatively balanced on the surface: 33 percent of the staffers were white, 36 percent were African American, and 31 percent were Latina. Most of the powerful and prestigious positions were held by whites, however; they were the clinicians, the directors of all the units, and the center manager. The maternity care coordinators (or MCCs)—two Latinas and two whites—occupied a mid-level status. Most of the African American staff worked in lower-status positions such as receptionist, medical assistant, laboratory technician, WIC nutrition department coordinator, and nutritionist. Most of the Latinas also held a lower-status position, working as receptionist, client-care coordinator, medical assistant, laboratory technician, WIC administrative assistant, and pharmacy assistant. There were exceptions at the top. The executive director, whose office was not on-site, was an African American man. An African American female clinician initially worked at Care Inc. two days a week, but she soon quit to go into private practice. An African American woman held the position of lead nurse.

As mentioned above, at Care Inc. white employees dominated the higher-status and higher-paid jobs in the clinic (such as the clinicians and unit directors), while Latinas and African American women per-formed the majority of lower-paid jobs (such as medical assistants and receptionists) requiring fewer skills. This was representative of the larger, split labor market, where African American and Latina/o workers hold fewer high-paying jobs, which are generally taken by white workers (Bonacich 1972; Conley 1999; Giddens 2001; Grusky and Sorensen 1998; Horowitz 1997; Wilson 1978, 1987, 1996). This stratified, race/class system is evident, in part, in the elevated levels of poverty among oppressed racial and ethnic groups (Bonacich 1972; Wilson 1987, 1996). Stratification—by race, ethnic-ity, or sex—creates divisions among workers and weakens their power against higher-ups, making collective action on the part of rank-and-file workers more difficult (Feagin 1991; Wilson 1978, 1987, 1996).

3

Threats to Moral Identity and Disparity in "Moral" Wages

IN THIS SECTION I DESCRIBE some structural inequalities present within Care Inc. that made the job more challenging and less fulfilling for some of the staff. These structural inequalities included the training and supervision of Latina staff by the more senior African American staff; the "gatekeeping" positions several of the African American women held that gave them some power over the mostly Latina/o clients (i.e., the African American triage nurse and the African American receptionist had the power to decide who could see a provider); and the attempts by some African American staffers to require that all staff members speak only English when not directly interacting with Spanish-speaking clients.

Workplace Inequalities at Care Inc.

All of the staffers at Care Inc. worked under challenging conditions. They sacrificed prestige within the local community because most of their clients were poor (often undocumented) Latinas/os; their work did not bestow them with social prestige (Goffman, 1961, 1974). The clients' race, ethnicity, and class can, as Goffman put it, "spoil" the health-care practitioners' identity (Goffman 1961). This is particularly true in North Carolina, where many citizens and members

44

of the legislature see poor Latinas/os as lower-status immigrants, undeserving of services (Hemming, Rouveral, and Hornsby 2001; Hyde and Leiter 2000). In particular, the Latina staffers of lower- and mid-level status often talked about unsympathetic legislators who gave the clinic's clients low priority. In a staff meeting, Rachel, the supervisor of the maternity care coordinators, complained: "We can only put out fires, there is no preventive care. We do not have the time or staff. The problem is of course that I cannot convince the legislature to give us money and the resources we need. They don't care about the population we serve. They are full of bigotry. They don't care about Hispanics because they cannot vote. Thus, there are no grants, no support, and no money" (Fieldnotes).

All the Latina staffers claimed that many US citizens disliked Latinas/os, defining them as threats to US values. For example, the maternity care coordinators often cited the visit by David Duke, head of the National Organization for European American Rights, who came to a neighboring town, Siler City, North Carolina, and denounced Mexicans, immigrants, and other minorities as threats to national unity (Anti-Defamation League 2006). The lower- and mid-level Latina health-care workers saw the plight of this unpopular clientele as a challenge and a call to action.

Without exception, all of the clinic staff felt overwhelmed by the speed-up necessitated by the relentless daily volume of people they served. All the health-care workers experienced work overload and complained to each other (and to me) about it. It was common for them to keep track of the clients seen in a day and to compare it to "their record." For example, when I began my fieldwork, the African American triage nurse frequently gave me an update, such as: "Today I saw 88 clients. Very close to my all-time record of 98 clients." However, as noted above, given the layout of the clinic, the lower-status staff members (African Americans and Latinas) were in direct contact with the clients, while the white higher-status staff had more physical separation from clients. This direct contact, coupled with the high volume of clients, rendered the jobs of African American and Latina staffers more stressful.

Mid- and lower-status staff in all the units I observed performed several tasks at once, faced a constant flow of clients coming in for services, and managed to meet more expectations than they could reasonably be expected to fulfill. The African American medical assistant, whom I call "Eva," recalled in an interview:

> It's a lot of work. It's a lot of work you have to do that you're not compensated for. My job, it's like, oh, my God, I can't believe it! My job goes from being a medical assistant and if medical records needs some help "we want you all to go in and help medical records." They want you to help medical records till now the senior manager has added a form inside the patient's chart because the address is not correct. So, now we have to do billing and ask the patient "Is this your correct address or what is your correct address?" that should be part of when a patient checks in. So now they've put that on there. So, our jobs go from one thing to another. You know what I'm saying? It's always something. Always. Mm hmm.

Similarly, one of the two receptionists told me, "the pace is relentless." The receptionist, for example, answered the phone (which rang constantly), took a message or transferred a call to a staff member in one of the units of the clinic, and attended to the person in line who either had an appointment with a doctor or might need a follow-up appointment, while, at the same time, she worked on the computer, printed an encounter form (containing the client information used by the billing department to determine fees), made copies of the insurance cards (i.e., Medicaid, Medicare, or private insurance), looked for the medical charts of clients that came in as walk-ins, and highlighted the name of the client in the schedule as a way of verifying that all the scheduled clients had shown up. The bilingual receptionist, in addition to her usual tasks, translated as needed for the triage nurse, the pharmacist, and the person in charge of medical records. This went on all day, five days a week. As I wrote in my fieldnotes when I worked as a volunteer in that job:

> I feel I am on a treadmill, and that the speed it is on is too fast for me. I have too many things to do—even at the same time!—and I never seem to finish doing something before I have something else to do or someone else to help. Only once

today I had a break around 6:30 p.m., when no one was in line and the phone was not ringing. I took a deep breath. I needed to catch my breath, and this was the first time I had the time to do so. I had not even taken a bathroom break, and I had been working for more than five and a half hours straight! At this time I remember thinking I had more than an hour to go, since today I had been scheduled to volunteer from 1 p.m. to 8 p.m. I had one and a half more hours! I am hungry, tired, stressed, and my head is buzzing. Am I going to make it?

If the computers were down (the computers are connected to a network and share a program where all client information is kept), or the printer did not work or was out of paper, or if the photocopy machine was being used by someone else, or if a co-worker was sick or on vacation, or if children were crying or running around the clinic, or if there were more clients than usual, the receptionists' daily work became even more taxing and stressful. The work became "terrible" and often "unbearable" if co-workers were out sick or on vacation. Margaret, the African American receptionist, explained in an interview that a bad day for her was when employees "have called out": "If you don't have enough employees here, if one or two or three have called out and you're trying to do registration, front desk, answer the phone, check people in, all at one time, which you can't do, and then with all the other disturbances, that's a bad day to me."

At a staff meeting, lower-status staff said that they were "stressed out" and that the situation "is made worse when staff is out or positions are vacant." The WIC director described the situation, in a memo sent to the administrators and unit directors (and noting that this could be shared with anyone):

> It was clear from the staff meeting that [the clinic's] staff are feeling stressed by the staff shortages (medical assistant, registrar, and pending Center Manager). Staff is working with a minimal level of staffing as it is, so that when staff is out or positions are vacant, a stressful situation is made worse. This is clearly noted in the breakdown of the registration system. . . . The center needs the support of administration to see that

these positions are filled as soon as possible. In addition, the underlying causes of the high turnover of center managers at this center needs to be investigated.

Understaffing and high turnover were not the only problems staff complained about. Several mid- and lower-status staff members, especially single mothers, often griped about their meager pay and the problems they faced making ends meet. It was not uncommon to find them glancing at their checking account balance, listing the bills they had to pay, and deciding which ones they could pay and which ones would have to wait until the next payday. The majority of the lower-status staff held two jobs. This was understandable. For example, at Care Inc. in 2002, a recently hired medical assistant (I) was paid $17,200 a year, and a medical assistant (II) was paid $18,900. A licensed practical nurse was paid a little more (between $19,700 and $28,700). Maternity care coordinators were paid $26,000 a year, and the registered nurse, $31,000. Medical assistants working at a private practice or firm earn, on average, $26,605 a year, while a licensed practical nurse is paid $33,054 year, and a registered nurse $49,987 a year. (Care Inc.'s chief financial officer supplied these salary approximations.) Many lower-status staff held part-time jobs at night or weekend jobs. They worked at local nursing homes as nurses' aides or at a local hospital as medical assistants. Without sufficient monetary compensation, they sought other avenues of value from their work at Care Inc. These are the conditions under which the staffers are driven to develop a moral identity.

Although the jobs were low paying, the lower-status Latina and African American women on staff needed them. They were the best these staffers could hope for. Also, affordable health-care services in the community were at a premium. The clientele needed health care, but there was not enough to go around. For the white higher-status staff, their skills and credentials ensured they could find jobs elsewhere. To them, working at Care Inc. was thus an opportunity to give back to the community: they earned an additional "moral" wage, consisting of esteem from their friends, family, and colleagues. The idea of a "moral" wage is related to W. E. B. Du Bois's concept of a "psychic wage": he argued that, during Reconstruction, low-class whites would accept low wages from white elites in exchange for community esteem and freedom from constant violence: "It must be remembered that the white group of laborers, while they received a low wage, were compensated in part by a sort of public and psychological wage. They were given public deference and titles of courtesy because they were white. They were admitted freely with all classes of white people to public functions, public parks, and the best schools" ([1935] 1998, 700).

The lower-status Latina and African American staff may also have been doing "moral" work, but their needs were more immediate: they needed the money these jobs provided, and they needed to make sure their own community (race) received the services they needed at the clinic. As Eva, the African American medical assistant, said in an interview: "I have no plans at this moment of going anywhere. I would like, I mean, you know, I'm not going to say I don't have any plans, but I would like to go maybe to another clinic that pays more money because working at the clinic that I'm in does not pay that well. It does not pay much money, you know. I'm gaining wonderful experience and that's what I want. . . . I mean, but it's OK."

Besides salaries, other structural inequalities at the clinic can be divided into three general parts: the rule of seniority; the perpetuation of gatekeepers; and the attempt to exclude Spanish language from the lunchroom and from the workplace when not speaking directly with clients.

The Rule of Seniority

At Care Inc., Latina and African American staff occupied lower-status positions. However, because of seniority, African American staffers trained and supervised Latina staffers. Latina staffers assumed that African American staffers had more power and advantages than Latina staffers. They criticized African American staffers for being authoritarian and making more work for them by asking them to translate. Latina staffers also argued that administrators cared more about African American staffers' needs, and that African American clients had other options for jobs, health care, and other social services that Latina/o clients lacked because they were not US citizens (unlike the African American clientele). As a result, Latina staffers claimed that African American women were more powerful both inside and outside of Care Inc.

The Latina staff frequently told me: "Black staff have not been able to work together with us and get the job done"; "They criticize us to the directors or supervisors"; and "They act like our bosses." When I worked with the receptionists (whom I have called Tatiana and Margaret), I wrote the following in my fieldnotes: "[Tatiana] is the new Latina receptionist. [Margaret] is teaching her how to use the computers. [Tatiana] said 'I know nothing about computers. I have years of not working on this, but I am going to give it all I've got.' After [Tatiana] asked [Margaret] two or three times how something was done, [Margaret] said in an annoyed tone: 'I already explained it to you once: Where're your notes?' "

Margaret had little patience to train Tatiana and teach her to use the computer. Like any new employee, Tatiana would be in jeopardy of losing her job if she did not learn how to do it. Without training, her efficiency suffered (subjecting her to the accusation of being "lazy"). A few months later, I asked Tatiana: "When you began working at the clinic, what was the hardest part about it?" She replied that it was dealing with the negative comments from the African American receptionist as she was learning her job.

Because they were not bilingual, the African American lower-status staffers relied on Latina staffers to translate for them. This organizational set-up was a source of tension. Latina staffers told me that African American staffers "took advantage of them" and bossed them around. Tatiana explained:

> Stephanie [the African American triage nurse] believes she is my boss. She says, "Come, help me translate. Can you hear me? Translate." I wanted to say to her, "Translate what? You don't even let people talk! So what do you want me to translate?". . . And when they asked Stephanie and Margaret [the African American receptionist] if they wanted to learn Spanish, Margaret said: "I'm not going to do extra. Because if they decide to come to a country where they don't speak, where people don't speak their language, it's their choice to pay the consequence." And she would start saying ugly things.

> Stephanie se cree mi jefa. Ella decía, "Ven a ayudarme a translate. Can you hear me? Translate." Yo quería decirle, "Translate

what? You don't even let people talk! So what do you want for me to translate?". . . Y cuando le preguntaron a Stephanie y a Margaret si querían aprender español, Margaret dijo: "I'm not going to do extra. Because if they decide to come to a country where they don't speak, where people don't speak their language, it's their choice to pay the consequence." Y empezaba a decir cosas feas. (Interview)

The African American staff did not treat translation as a skill crucial to their work, but as an inconvenience that Latina workers should have to deal with. From my fieldnotes, I found that many of the African American staffers regarded translation as a hassle and not part of their skill set. This might have been a way for African American staffers to protect themselves, because Care Inc. did not offer free, on-the-job language lessons so that the African American staff could learn Spanish. African American staffers felt threatened by the influx of Spanish-speaking staff because the Latinas possessed this valuable skill. As a result, the African American staff resented Spanish speaking as a crutch for "lazy" people (Latina/o clients) who should "pay the consequence" for "choosing" not to learn English.

Latina staffers often told me that African American staffers treated other African American staff members well, but bossed around the Latinas. During my fieldwork I, too, observed that African American staffers interacted differently with other African American staffers than with the Latina staff. I wrote in my fieldnotes: "As clients arrive, Eva [African American medical assistant] says to Barbara and Bibiana [Latina medical assistants], 'Are you hurrying? I am taking notes!' Meanwhile, Eva is seated, talking on the phone with her husband. A few minutes later, as Barbara started to fill out some paperwork, Eva said to Barbara, in front of a client: 'Look at that paper, no, no, watch it, that is not the way it is done.' "

I never saw Eva hurry up Genesis, the other African American medical assistant. Eva only did this with the Latina medical assistants. I asked Barbara, the Latina medical assistant, about this, and she said:

Ay. I'm telling you, I do not get along with Eva. How can I explain it to you? I have learned to put up with her. . . . Eva is bossy. She wants to boss you around, as if she was your supervisor. . . . And if you say anything to her, she gets fierce; in other words, you have gained an enemy. . . . But I have realized that that is her way. . . . No, with Genesis she does not do it.

Ay. Yo te digo, yo no me voy con Eva. Eva ya yo, ¿cómo te digo? Ya aprendí a sobrellevarla. . . . Eva es mandona. Te quiere mangonear, como si ya fuera la supervisora. . . . Y que si tú le dices, se pone como que una fiera, que mejor dicho, consigues una enemiga. . . . Pero yo me he dado cuenta de que eso es su manera de ser de ella. No, con Genesis no lo hace. (Interview)

A few times, Latina staffers complained to the (higher level) white staff about the African American staff. Stephanie, the African American triage nurse, was eventually fired after Latina/o clients complained about her to the center manager, the lead clinician, and the human resources coordinator. But, as the record in Stephanie's case shows, the clients and the Latina staff were not listened to right away. It took several months and frequent complaints from clients and Latina staffers before she was reprimanded. Only after the director of an allied Hispanic organization documented the complaints he received about Care Inc. from Latina/o clients was Stephanie asked to meet with the lead clinician and strongly encouraged to "change." Stephanie was fired only after she denied a (white) girl access to see a clinician and, a few minutes later, the girl convulsed and had to be sent to a local hospital.

Latina staff asserted that the African American staff had control over Latinas in this setting. However, it is necessary to point out that African American staffers were not the privileged members of Care Inc. African American staff members, like the Latina staff, were only trying to hold on to what status they had managed to gain. African American staffers did have a better position structurally (in terms of Care Inc.'s workplace organization) than Latina staffers, but they were still vulnerable within Care Inc.'s management, where the most powerful positions were held by whites. African American women who did not speak or understand Spanish were, in fact, in jeopardy of losing their jobs. The African American staff mentioned to me that if they were looking for a job at the clinic today, they would not be hired, because they did not speak Spanish. They also told me that if a staff person had to be let go, it would most likely be a lower-status, non-Spanish-speaking staff member. And they were correct in believing that Latinas who could speak Spanish would be more likely to be hired than African Americans; their fears were not unfounded. From the time I began my fieldwork, all the new employees were Latinas or Spanish speakers; being fluent in Spanish was a skill noted as important in the job listings.

Gatekeepers

Several African American women held positions that gave them some "gatekeeping" power over clients. For example, the African American triage nurse and the African American receptionist had the power to decide who could see a provider. The triage nurse saw all patients who came without an appointment to Care Inc. She decided who would be seen that day and who would have to come back—or give up. During my time at Care Inc., I observed that she often used this power selectively, using it to deny Latina/o clients access to health-care professionals. I noticed how the triage nurse, after asking some Latina patients their symptoms or those of their children, would tell them that their ailments did not merit seeing a doctor and would not fill out the form giving them permission to see a doctor. She told me that the Latinas/os "work the system" and at times sought unnecessary medical care for their children by lying or getting their children to lie.

Other Latina staffers also reported that the African American triage nurse used her gatekeeping powers against Latina/o patients. This is illustrated by the following conversation between two Latina maternity care coordinators, whom I have called Yolanda and MariaTe:

> *Yolanda:* You know, MariaTe, it gets more and more difficult to work here. . .
> *MariaTe:* What happened?
> *Yolanda:* The triage nurse [an African American woman] doesn't let me talk or do my job. She "shushed" me. She did not let me talk. I wanted one of my patients to see the doctor.

The only thing she told me was that if she [Latina patient] wanted to see someone right away, if she could not wait, she should go to the ER. . . . They don't want us to do our job. What for, if most of our clients are Hispanic? Our work does not count because our clients do not count. We are only here to be a nuisance to them. We are an imposition.

Yolanda: Sabes MariaTe, cada vez esta más pesado trabajar . . .
MariaTe: ¿Qué pasó?
Yolanda: La triage nurse no me deja hablar y no me deja hacer mi trabajo. Me cayó. No me dejó contarle nada. Quería que una de mis pacientes viera a la doctora. Solo me dijo que si ella [paciente Latina] quería ver a alguien inmediatamente, si no podía esperar, que se fuera a emergencias. . . . No quieren que uno haga su trabajo. ¿Para qué, si la mayoría de nuestras pacientes son hispanas? Nuestro trabajo no cuenta, porque nuestras pacientes no cuentan. Solo estamos aquí para molestar. Somos una imposición. (Fieldnotes)

The receptionists were also "gatekeepers"; clients were obliged to talk to them in order to get an appointment with a doctor. I observed many instances when the African American receptionist told a Latina/o patient to call later because she did not speak Spanish. Margaret, the African American receptionist, often forwarded a Latina/o patient's call to Tatiana, the Latina receptionist, whose line was often busy with other calls. If Latina/o clients did call back, they were told by Margaret, the African American receptionist, that there were no more appointments available for that month. Margaret also often put the Latinas/os who were new to the clinic on a three- or four-month waiting list to see a doctor. Latina staffers noticed this as well. The Latina WIC assistant, Mariana, told me in an interview:

Margaret [the African American receptionist] sometimes really annoys me. She is working at the front desk with Tatiana [Latina receptionist] who has so many people waiting for her, and Margaret, mockingly, answers the phone: "English? Spanish, Spanish. There's nothing I can do." And she starts reading her magazines, cleaning her glasses, and putting on lipstick.

One day I asked Tatiana: "Can I help you?" She answers: "No, no, thank you." And Margaret asks me: "You need anything, honey?" she asked me, that way. And I replied: "No, I am asking Tatiana if she needs help." And Margaret responds: "Oh no, it's just for her. It's Spanish, Spanish. You know."

Esta Margaret, a veces me cae muy mal. Porque a veces está trabajando el front desk y esta Tatiana [recepcionista Latina] tiene tanta gente esperándola y Margaret como burlándose contesta el teléfono: "English? Spanish, Spanish. There's nothing I can do." Y se pone a leer sus revistas y se pone a limpiar sus lentes, y se pone a pintar los labios. Un día le dije a Tatiana "¿Te ayudo?" Dice: "No, no gracias." Y me dice Margaret: "You need anything, honey?" me dijo a mí, así. Y le dije: "No. Estoy preguntando a Tatiana que si necesita ayuda." Me responde Margaret, "Oh, no, it's just for her. It's Spanish, Spanish. You know."

Margaret was frequently described as acting in a disdainful manner toward Latina/o clients. Latina staffers mentioned to me how Margaret would often put Latinas/os on a waiting list and limit Latina/o clients access to care by ignoring calls by Spanish-speaking clients looking to schedule a visit with a doctor.

Konrad et al. (1998) found that in private practices, staff often blocked particular patients' access to doctors. In their study, actors who played mothers who had insurance, mothers who were uninsured, or mothers on Medicaid were treated quite differently. Medicaid and uninsured patients had the most difficulty getting help for their children. Staff members' negative attitudes toward these patients amplified and reinforced the financial and non-financial barriers to health care already faced by uninsured and Medicaid patients. This study suggests that receptionists' views about a stigmatized or oppressed group can determine whether members of that group get care or not.

This power without status or pay is in many ways a limited power; it is hard to see how African American people actually benefit from denying Latinas/os health care. But in a context of limited and shrinking resources, such as at Care Inc., this can seem like real power at the clinic, even if it has only short-term effects.

Attempts to Exclude Spanish
Language from the Workplace

As of 2002, Care Inc. served mainly Latinas/os. As stated earlier, the changing demographics at the clinic reflect the fact that within the last 20 years North Carolina has seen a high rate of Latina/o immigration. African American female staffers interpreted these demographic changes as evidence that Latinas/os were "taking over" the clinic, and that African American clients' interests and needs were no longer a priority because the "clinic is catering to Latinas/os."

As Care Inc.'s clientele changed, clinic administrators hired bilingual workers to replace departing staff. Most new staffers (95 percent) were Latinas who spoke Spanish and English (and were willing to take a low-paying job at a community clinic). African American female staff felt threatened by this situation. For example, six of them said to me on separate occasions: "I can't understand many of the clients who come into the clinic and so I feel unable to help those clients. I feel that my Spanish-speaking co-workers perceive me as useless"; "In situations where my co-workers are discussing problems in Spanish, I feel frustrated by the thought that I could be useful if only I understood [or] if they spoke English"; "I feel I wouldn't be hired at this company right now because I don't speak Spanish. This makes me feel even more useless"; "I feel excluded from groups of Spanish speaking co-workers"; "I feel insulted when people speak a language I can't understand in front of me; I feel like they are talking about me. I feel disrespected"; and "The presence of a staff that is mostly bilingual and the decision to hire bilingual people as often as possible has led to a clinic that is welcoming to Hispanics but can be perceived as pushing away other target people. I miss the old client population at the clinic—my friends and family used to come here and now they do not." Not being able to identify or effectively communicate with their new clientele, these African American women searched for ways to make sense of, and respond to, their declining status.

In a staff meeting, the lead doctor, a white woman who I'll call Dr. Koncord, had suggested that English be spoken all the time. Non-Spanish-speaking staff members (in particular African American, lower-status staffers) had complained to Dr. Koncord that they felt disrespected, criticized, and made fun of because they did not know or were not willing to learn Spanish. Latina staffers, including Amanda (the client-care coordinator) and Tatiana (the receptionist), complained to me that they were now "prohibited to speak Spanish." To the Latinas, the one valuable skill they possessed was being devalued.

Although Latinas and African American staffers occupied roughly the same low-level positions, most African American staffers had been working at the clinic for many years and had seniority relative to Latina staff. The Latinas had been hired in the last few years, largely as a result of the high Latina/o immigration rate to North Carolina. Of the forty employees working at Care Inc. in 2002, 32.5 percent were white, 35 percent were African American, and 30 percent were Latinas. Again, this represented a fairly dramatic demographic shift compared to the mid-1990s, when the majority of the staff was African American.

Latina staff told me that they suffered indignities at the hands of the African American staff (but not the white staff). For a Latina nutritionist, Catalina, Latina workers were not a priority at the clinic. She said:

> They require the people who speak Spanish not to speak Spanish at the clinic, even during their lunch break. I don't know what the hell they are doing. . . . Even during lunch hour? Why? . . . Because they feel discriminated against, but that is not discrimination. If you prohibit someone who is Hispanic from speaking Spanish . . . that is also discrimination. Nowhere in the world can they prohibit you from speaking a language. . . . What is going on in the clinic that they would decide to make this a topic of discussion during the staff meeting?

> Ellas requieren que las personas que hablan español, no hablen español en la clínica, incluso en sus horas del almuerzo. No sé qué carajo están haciendo. . . . ¿Aun en la hora del almuerzo? ¿Por qué? . . . se sienten discriminadas, pero eso no es discriminación. Si tú prohíbes a una persona hispana que hable español . . . eso sí es discriminación. En ninguna parte del mundo pueden prohibir que tú hables una lengua. . . . ¿Qué pasa en la clínica para que se venga a poner ese asunto como un punto del orden del día?

Catalina tried to answer the question she had posed:

> You know what bothers me? You know what it is? The priorities
> they have. The priority is to do everything so the people who
> do not speak Spanish, especially the black people, do not feel
> bad. That bothers me.

> ¿Sabes lo que me molesta? ¿Sabes lo que es? Es las prioridades
> que tienen. La prioridad es hacer todo para que no se molesten
> las personas que no hablan español, en especial los morenos.
> Eso me molesta. (Interview)

Other Latina staff echoed Catalina's discontent over what Dr.
Koncord had said. Amanda, the patient-care coordinator, confided
in me:

> They don't want us to speak Spanish, unless it is work related.
> . . . What if the shoe was on the other foot, if it was the other
> way around? It is the opinion of the morenas [African American
> women], in particular [the receptionist], that "all the Hispan-
> ics have to learn English." But, why shouldn't she learn our
> Spanish? And if it bothers her so much, and she refuses to learn
> Spanish, why is she working here? Her job is to deal with all the
> clients, and here it is Hispanic and American clients. And it so
> happens that the majority of the clients now are Hispanic. . . .
> And if you think about it, it is five morenas [African American
> women] in particular who do not speak Spanish.

> No quieren que hablemos más en español, al menos que sea por
> trabajo. . . . ¿Qué si fuera al revés, si fuera de la otra manera?
> Es la opinión de las morenas, y en particular la opinión de [la
> recepcionista], que: "todos los hispanos tienen que aprender
> inglés." ¿Pero, por qué no debe ella aprender nuestro español?
> ¿Y si la incomoda tanto, y ella rechaza aprender español, por
> qué está ella trabajando aquí? Su trabajo es el servir a todos los
> pacientes, y aquí los pacientes son hispanos y americanos. Y
> sucede que ahora, aquí, la mayoría de los pacientes son hispanos.

. . . Y si tú lo piensas, son cinco morenas, en particular, que no hablan español. (Fieldnotes)

When the Latina staff complained to higher-status white staff, they were usually unable to effect change, and, according to the Latinas, white staff saw them as troublemakers.

The responsibility for the problem shifted from Dr. Koncord (who made the decision) to the African American staff (who had filed the complaint). Blaming the African American women made sense in a context where they were seen as "pushy" and could force people (even whites) to accept their demands. This also reinforced the belief among the Latinas that the African American women on staff could not be true victims of racism because they could impose their will and receive preferential treatment from white administrators. When the Latina staff went to Dr. Koncord, they felt relatively powerless. For example, when Tatiana, the Latina receptionist, complained to Dr. Koncord about the African American receptionist's behavior, Tatiana said she got the cold shoulder:

> *Tatiana:* I said to Dr Koncord, "She is very rude with Hispanic people." I said to her, "I do not know if she is rude with everyone. But I have seen her act rude only with Latinos."
> *Natalia:* What happened?
> *Tatiana:* For a good while the doctor did not talk to me. We would only greet one another, "Good morning." But a month later she asked me again how things were, and I said to her, "What do you need to know? Nothing has changed since I talked to you. What do you want to know?" I was very annoyed, you know.

> *Tatiana:* Yo le dije a Dr. Koncord, "Ella es muy grosera con la gente latina." Le dije, "No sé si es grosera con todo el mundo. Pero yo la he visto ser grosera solo con los latinos."
> *Natalia:* ¿Y qué pasó?
> *Tatiana:* Por un buen rato la doctora ni me hablaba. Solo nos decíamos "Good morning." Pero un mes después ella volvió a preguntarme como estaban las cosas, yo le dije, "What do

you need to know? Nothing has changed since I talked to you. What do you want to know?" Yo estaba muy molesta, sabes. (Fieldnotes)

After the staff meeting, one of the Latina medical assistants told me what she would have liked to have said in front of all the staff, but was afraid to: "Sorry, Dr. Koncord, but we know our rights and we know we got the right to talk Spanish, anything we wanted to talk that is not work-related. Nobody is going to take that away from us. No one" (Fieldnotes).

Latina workers complained that the higher-status white staff and administrators prioritized the African American staff's needs and wants. As a result, Latina staffers claimed that their own needs were secondary to those of the African American staff. Dr. Koncord might have been trying to appease unhappy staff without realizing the history of racial tension among the lower-status staff. The Latinas interpreted Dr. Koncord's actions as an example of African American women's influence, acting pushy and imposing their will on others (even whites, such as Dr. Koncord). If African American women could force white administrators to change policies, the Latinas felt that African Americans' claim of being victims of racism rang hollow.

In sum, working conditions—low pay, overwork, low prestige, and high staff turnover—threatened health-care practitioners' moral identity. In addition, however, these difficulties within the clinic made the job more challenging and less fulfilling for some of the staff, in particular the lower- and mid-status Latina staff and the lower-status African American staff. Structural inequalities—training and supervision of Latina staff by the more senior African American staff, the "gatekeeping" positions held by several of the African American women, and the pressure by some African American staff to ban Spanish from the workplace—also threatened the crafting of a moral identity by staffers at Care Inc.

4

Moral Identity and Racial Solidarity

How Lower-Status Workers Fashion a Superior Self

FEMINISTS OF COLOR HAVE MADE A CASE for the need to understand how numerous identities—race, ethnicity, gender, class, and nationality—are experienced in daily life, and how these identities intersect and shape each other. Intersectional feminist theorists contend that identities are fashioned by the multiple, interconnected oppressed and privileged groups to which we belong (e.g., Anzaldúa and Moraga 2002). Intersectional theorists "view race, class, gender, sexuality, ethnicity, and age, among others, as mutually constructing systems of power. [And] . . . these systems permeate all social relations" (Collins 2000, 11).

Intersectional theory in this study calls for an analysis of how health-care practitioners' positions within multiple, interlocking systems of inequality shape their understandings of themselves and their construction of a moral identity. In the following analysis I explore the ways health-care workers' race, class, and nationality contribute to their fashioning of a morally superior self. I highlight how intersectionality works "on the ground" and plays out in the everyday interactions of these health-care practitioners.

61

The Lower-Status African American Staffers

Several of the lower-status African American staffers had worked in the health-care industry for many years, although they had been working at Care Inc. for only a couple of years. Margaret, for example, the African American receptionist, had retired from University Hospital (a major local hospital) after working there for 30 years and had been working at Care Inc. for "three years. Three long years." Eva, the African American medical assistant, had been a nursing assistant for 20 years and a medical assistant for three years. When I asked her how she decided to become a nursing assistant and medical assistant, she elaborated in an interview:

> I guess, growing up, I grew up being an asthmatic child. So, just being around a lot of people that, you know, that worked on me and helped me in my life. That's probably why I chose to do what I do now. . . . My first job was at . . . a nursing home . . . that's where I got my training. And that was a very good experience, you know, because I had no clue to what nurse's duties were until I started doing it. And I mean, this is very good. I enjoy it, I really do. I enjoy working with people and helping people.

For the majority of the lower-status African American female staff, the work felt less rewarding due to the changing demographics at the clinic. Language barriers made the African American staff feel "useless," "frustrated," "excluded," "insulted," and "disrespected," and prompted one of them to wonder if the bilingual issue was not "pushing away other target people." Not being able to identify or effectively communicate with their new clientele, these African American women searched for ways to make sense of, and respond to, their declining status.

At the same time, the African American staff felt comfortable with the African American patients who came into the clinic. For example, Margaret, the African American receptionist, knew the African American patients' names, complimented the women by saying things like, "What a nice dress you have on today, and perfect for this weather." She usually greeted them warmly and talked and laughed with them for a while. This behavior was in marked contrast to her interactions with whites and Latina/os. A possible explanation for her familiarity with the African American clients might have been that she knew African American clients from her neighborhood, church, or another community organization; however, Margaret had recently moved from New York to North Carolina, and she said that she didn't know many people. Even if they weren't personal acquaintances, African American clients apparently increased her comfort and sense of value within the clinic. Without African American clientele, she perceived that she would not be needed in her job.

In this section I analyze how gendered and racialized frames shaped the way the African American health-care providers crafted a moral identity. The strategies—defining the lower-status Latina health-care staff as lazy and defining Latinas as bad mothers and as abusing the health-care system—drew on racial, class, and nationalist frames. The African American staffers' master narrative about the moral self—the moral health-care worker and the moral client—categorized Latinas as "bad" for "working the system," and labeled them as irresponsible care-seekers who were undeserving of subsidized health care in the United States, whereas they perceived African American women as "good" workers, mothers, and clients. The construction of their moral identity relied on racial solidarity rhetoric.

Lazy Latinas

The African American staff at times defined the Latina staff as "lazy." As Margaret, the African American receptionist, said: "[Latina staff] have not been able, or willing, as some are saying, to get the job done." Five African American staff members described Latina staffers as troublemakers and "whiners" who constantly complained about their workload.

Margaret said in an interview:

> I think the company doesn't hire a lot of people with good work ethics. You know what I'm saying? To me, anything goes here. This place is too laid back. . . . I mean, you know, if there are rules, then they need to be abided by. Here it just seems to me, and I know there are rules and regulations, but it just doesn't

seem they are enforced. I think as far as like going on extended vacation, like a month or two because they're going out of the country, to their country, and their position is not replaced. That's hard on the person that's still here.

The African American staff members were frustrated by a workplace strategy that the Latina staff saw as their only option to travel home, which was time consuming. The Latina staff accrued vacation time and extended it by taking sick leave and planning their trips near holidays. These long vacations, however, made work difficult for the remaining workers at the already understaffed clinic. However, Margaret focused the blame only on the Latina staff, not on the center manager or administrators who approved these vacation arrangements.

The African American women on staff were also frustrated by the speed of the Latina workers. The senior African American medical assistant felt she needed to prod the Latina staff constantly:

> *Eva:* The hardest thing is when my co-workers are not doing their 100 percent, not giving their all. And that happens when I'm working and working and working and working, trying to do ten million things and it's just impossible and your co-workers are not pitching in. That's pretty bad.
> *Natalia:* How do you deal with that?
> *Eva:* I am the lead medical assistant there, and so, my thing, which they don't like, I don't stay on them, but I do kind of remind them, you know, that this is what they're supposed to do, you know: "trabajen rápido [work fast]." You know? I have to remind them that if they're going to work here we got to work together. This is the only way it's going to work, is together. (Interview)

Eva implies that Latinas are choosing not to work fast enough: only a neglectful worker needs to be reminded to keep up. By prompting co-workers to work faster in broken Spanish, Eva implies that Latinas are the lazy, ineffective workers at Care Inc. Similarly, Genesis (an African American medical assistant) and Desiree (the African American lead nurse) criticized the Latina medical assistants, Barbara and

Bibiana, who worked with them in the clinical area. I often heard Genesis commenting to Desiree that "Barbara is very slow. Very slow! She doesn't do what she is supposed to do." It is worth noting that Barbara, a recently hired medical assistant, was supposed to be trained by Desiree or Genesis. However, after working for six months at Care Inc., Barbara had not been trained to do all the procedures she was expected to do. Even so, Desiree and Genesis put the onus on Barbara, not acknowledging that they were responsible for training her. In forming their moral identities, Desiree and Genesis did not see the irony in neglecting to train Barbara, given the historic stereotype of African Americans as unproductive after being denied workplace resources to succeed (Clawson and Trice 2000; Collins 2004; Gilens 1996, 1999).

Not all Latinas were labeled lazy, however. They treated me, as well as the higher-status Latina staff in another clinic department (e.g., maternity care coordinators), in a friendly and cordial manner. They praised us for our "hard work" and "dedication." Margaret told me: "You have been a blessing yourself this year, don't laugh, all over the clinic. I never once . . . whenever I ask you to . . . you know, call you on the intercom. 'Can you do so and so?' Never once did I hear, 'No, I'm busy.' I mean, you're always willing. And that's the kind of people they need to make things flow" (Interview).

The maternity care coordinators and I, however, all shared a common trait: a higher social class. We had educational credentials, were fluent in English, and had assimilated US cultural norms. Our jobs were "easier" because we had the tools to accomplish them. Our success also confirmed their characterization of laziness as a personal choice: one could choose to work hard, or not. We were the hard-working exceptions that proved the "lazy" rule. The African American staff looked at us as examples that Latinas/os *could* work harder, be dedicated, become assimilated, speak English, etc.

Further, the maternity care coordinators and I did not threaten the African American staff's social and economic status. As a PhD student and volunteer, I did not put their jobs in jeopardy. Rather, as a Spanish-English translator, I was a help, not a threat, to their jobs. The Latina maternity care coordinators also did not compete for the African American workers' jobs; all had graduated from a four-year college, and a couple had a graduate degree. As maternity care coordinators, they had education and training that put them in a different occupational category than the lower-status African American staff.

Bad Mothers and Unruly Children

Some in the African American staff also characterized Latina clients as "bad mothers." These African American staffers, as well as African American clients, constantly asserted that Latina clients must learn to teach their children to be quiet and sit still. For almost two weeks, Margaret (an African American woman who did not speak Spanish) and I worked as the clinic receptionists. She hushed Latina/o children running around the waiting area with a loud and angry "Shhhhhh!" If the child did not stop she would order the mother (or caretaker): "[She/he] is going to have to go." She barked and gestured roughly at clients. At first I thought she behaved this way with all the clients, but then I noticed that her demeanor changed when the clients were African American. As I wrote in my fieldnotes:

> Margaret seems to know the name of most of the African American people that come in. She also seems to be very friendly and willing (and able) to strike up conversations with them. "Hello, so-and-so, how are you doing today?" "I like that top you are wearing." "You went where for lunch? Did you get their biscuits?" "Hello, darling, how can I help you today?" However, with some whites and most Latinas/os she is rough, tough, impersonal, and cold. She seems not to know whites' or Latinas/os' names, and never calls them "sweetie," "darling," or "handsome" as she does with African American clients. To a Latino, for example, she barked "Need help?" When he did not reply she asked again, "Hey, need help?" She rolled her eyes and her voice became louder as she repeated herself. After the third time she said to me, "Natalia, check what is wrong with him."

Margaret also complained constantly about the noise the Latina/o children in the clinic made, saying, "Don't they know this is not a playground? They are driving me crazy!" On one occasion she remarked about three Latino five-year-olds, "Don't they go to school? You just see them so often that you start to wonder what they do all day."

When I interviewed Margaret, she said:

> The clinic is supposed to be for everybody. I guess that over the years, people, black and white clients, I mean, have just decided to go elsewhere because of the noise. It is a lot of children. . . . Hispanics is what I am speaking of; if one has an appointment you might see three or four people with them. There are not enough chairs to sit. There's a lot of noise. I've heard other clients say that, you know, they complain because there's not enough room, there's not enough chairs to sit, or there is too much noise in the waiting room and when you have older clients they don't want to hear all that noise and I can relate to that. If you're here and you're sick, you definitely don't want to hear it. . . . Mom or Dad has an appointment, you bring all the kids. School is open, your kid is here translating for you, missing school, and I don't know. . . . I guess because I've never seen that before until I started working here. Maybe it's allowed. It wouldn't be allowed with any of my children.

Here we see that Latina/o parents, and their "misbehaving" children, are cited as among the reasons why African American community members no longer visit the clinic. I often observed Latina clients bringing their children and other family members to the clinic when they came to see a clinician. Sometimes, Latinas would bring their older children along so that they could translate, watch the younger children during the parent's appointment, or take a younger child in for her/his appointment. Mothers often brought their children because they were responsible for taking care of them and did not have anyone with whom they could leave them (Chong 2002). Many Latina clients did not have extended family living in North Carolina (or in the United States). Again, Margaret described being a "bad mother" as a personal flaw unique to Latinas/os instead of a function of unaffordable child care options and limited translation services.

Margaret defined herself (and African Americans as a group) as different from and better than Latinas by emphasizing the differences (real or not) in parenting skills between African Americans and Latinas. She used defensive othering, a process by which one marginalized group constructs boundaries between itself and other marginalized groups, while at the same time defining its members as morally superior to these marginalized out-groups (Schwalbe et al. 2000).

It was also common for Stephanie, the African American triage nurse, to comment on Latinas' parenting; Latinos (the men) were rarely judged for their parenting abilities. On one occasion, Margaret shushed some Latina/o children who were laughing in the waiting room. She said to Stephanie and me, "I've got to fuss all day at these kids. They have no home training . . . Jesus!" On another occasion, Stephanie said to Margaret, in reference to some Latina/o children who were playing with a newspaper, "Where are these kids' mothers? We would never let our children behave like this." The "we," it seemed, were African American women. I recorded as fieldnotes the following conversation between Stephanie and Margaret. Stephanie said:

> A lot of children . . . come into the clinic. That's fine. But to me the parents don't have any control of their children. They don't seem to discipline their children. I mean, that's just my opinion. Because I see the kids doing things to their parents that I wouldn't allow; hitting them, or pulling them, telling them to stop, or no, or whatever. And there are certain places you go that children should be able to at least try to act, you know, good, or the parents should discipline them a little more as far as finding a way of keeping them quiet, some kind of way. I think that's a problem. And then I guess there are so many children that come in for WIC, for appointments, for walk-ins.

Most of the "parents" that Stephanie criticized were mothers who had brought their children with them to the clinic because they needed to be seen by a clinician, the WIC nutritionist, a maternity care coordinator, or other staff person at the clinic. What Margaret and Stephanie defined as uncontrollable and undisciplined children, Latina/o parents viewed as healthy, energetic, and happy children who were behaving as children should (Chong 2002). Because other children were at the clinic, Latina/o parents encouraged their children to play with them. If a child did not want to play or was "lethargic," Latina/o parents would take that as a sign that they were sick or coming down with something. As a Latina mother mentioned to me after being reprimanded by Stephanie:

> What does she have against my children? Thank God they are healthy, happy, and running around. Not like me, with a cold and pain all over my body. If children laugh or shout, she scolds us. Any noise puts her in a bad mood.

> ¿Qué tiene ella contra mis hijos? A Dios gracias de que ellos están bien, contentos y corriendo. No como yo, con gripa y dolor en todo el cuerpo. Si niños se ríen o gritan, ella nos regaña. Cualquier ruidito la pone de mal humor. (Fieldnotes)

Stephanie and Margaret did complain, on occasion, about the noise of African American and white children. But they rarely said anything to the African American or white parents, especially the mothers. Moreover, I never heard them label these mothers as bad. As I wrote in my fieldnotes:

> An African American woman, about 30 years old, came into the clinic today. She was first in the reception area, while waiting for her prescription to be filled, and then she came to the WIC office. Her five children accompanied her. Their ages were five, four, three, two, and less than one year old. Four of the children were girls. They were loud. While in the reception area and in the WIC office, I observed the children fighting, running around the offices, picking up pencils or paper on the desks, and dropping their jackets in the middle of the room. . . . The baby came to the desk where I was sitting, and started opening the drawers. The children shouted, and the mother shouted at them, once in a while, to be quiet. Yet, as the mother asked for silence, the children seemed to do just the opposite: cry, shout, or pull one of their siblings' hair to make her/him cry. . . . Stephanie said nothing to them when they were in the reception waiting room. No one at WIC said anything to them, either. But when the family left, Richard, the only African American staffer at WIC, called Stephanie and said: "Just called to tell you

that [she] was gone. They nearly tore up the place. I worked as fast as I could to get them out of here."

The African American staff did not regard this family as representative of African American families (Collins 1999). In fact, they seemed to silently rally to get this mother out the clinic doors without criticism. This stood in counterpoint to the way Latinas were confronted and criticized about their "unruly" children. After complaining to the mothers, Stephanie and Margaret typically commented that Latina mothers should do a better job of controlling their numerous children. However, they rarely complained or said anything to the African American mothers. And white mothers seemed beyond criticism. Cultural definitions of what constitutes "healthy" behavior will vary (Chong 2002). At Care Inc., however, these differences were accentuated and associated with racialized and gendered rhetoric that described Latinas as bad mothers. This cultural imagery fits seamlessly with prevailing explanations of why people of color experience high rates of crime, poverty, unemployment, etc. It places the blame on them and the way they behave, and not on the structural conditions that limit their opportunities (Solinger 2000; Williams 1995).

In the United States, motherhood is romanticized, and media portrayals "seem on the surface to celebrate motherhood, but in reality promulgate standards of perfection that are beyond . . . reach" (Douglas and Michaels 2004, 4–5). The media promote a white, middle-class ideal of motherhood that is difficult for any mother to live up to (Hays 1998); it is especially hard for poor women and women of color, who endure extra scrutiny and have few resources. The women who fail to meet these idealized standards are blamed "for being horrible rather than only human" (Caplan 1998, 127). Blaming individual mothers also negates the need to discuss why (and under what conditions) some mothers are "good."

Abusing the System

The African American staff put down Latinas by saying that they "worked the system," especially the health-care system, and were undeserving of services. Some of the behaviors African American staffers found acceptable for African American clients they found, conversely, unacceptable for Latina/o clients. For example, I observed the following encounter with Stephanie, the triage nurse: "An African American man and his teenage son came into Stephanie's office, asking to be seen by the doctor. They did not sit down, and when talking to Stephanie they did not look at her. When Stephanie asked for some details (i.e., how long the son had been sick, what was his temperature, etc.), the father rolled his eyes and sighed. Stephanie, although she did not get a response from him, did not ask twice, and wrote a note that allowed them to be seen by a doctor" (Fieldnotes).

Later that day,

> A Latina came into Stephanie's office with her two sons. She said to Stephanie, "Mi hijo está enfermo, ha tenido fiebre y no está comiendo [My son is sick, he has had a fever and he has not been eating.]" The mother did not sit down, as she was carrying the boy and holding onto the second son with her left hand. Stephanie asked "¿Cuánto temperatura? [What's his temperature?]" The mother replied, "No sé! [I do not know!]" Stephanie rolled her eyes, took her hand to the boy's forehead, and said, "Él bien. No fiebre. [He is OK, no fever.]" The mother and two sons walked out. (Fieldnotes)

The African American father was rude to Stephanie, but she did not comment on it, and let the man and his son see a doctor. The Latina mother attempted to communicate her distress to Stephanie, but Stephanie rolled her eyes and did not fill out the form to give permission for them to see a doctor. To Stephanie, Latinas appeared to be rude and uncooperative. She also maintained that Latinas/os feigned symptoms, or made their children feign symptoms, so that they would be seen by a clinician.

When Stephanie treated African American female clients, she was cordial and friendly. An African American client's visit with Stephanie often lasted twice as long as a Latina/o's visit with her. When asking about symptoms, Stephanie never challenged African American patients' accounts, as she did with Latina/o clients, and I never observed her deny an African American family access to medical care. She often commented to me, after a visit from an African

American client, that African Americans were fairly absent from the clinic because "they were driven away."

The African American staff often complained about giving health-care services to Latinas/os (Levenstein 2000). Margaret, the receptionist, complained about the "misuse" of the health-care system by the Latina/o clients. She said:

> I mean, sometimes it seems like some of the things they're coming in for they could remedy at home or figure it out yourself. Lord knows, if I came to the doctor every time I didn't feel good. . . . Especially, you know, allergies, your throat's sore, or whatever. It's allergies. . . . And I mean . . . we just seem to see a lot of clients . . . well, to me it seems like that . . . they come here also because they're not paying. They're not paying because we're one of the few that offer a sliding-fee scale, so you pay whatever that scale is. Or if you don't have any money, you have seen the doctor, you were here last week, it was the same thing. And that's allowed. . . . You know, it makes you think, well, I bet if they went to what I call a regular doctor's office and they did not offer a sliding fee scale, and they may have to pay that money, I mean, you know, some of these things they come in for, they wouldn't. (Interview)

Margaret made it clear that she, and by implication other African Americans, would not go to a clinician for trivial matters. She assumed that African American clients were more discerning than Latina/o clients; they knew when to use the clinic and when not to. The rhetoric of "abusing the system" has been used in the past to deny African American women ("welfare queens") social services as well (Adair 2000; Clawson and Trice 2000; Collins 2004; Gilens 1996, 1999; Jewell 1993; Roberts 1997, 2002). In both cases, it allows service providers a rationale for interpreting an action (visiting the clinic) as inspired by greed instead of need.

Other African American staff also criticized Latinas/os' use of the community clinic. Eva, the African American medical assistant, said:

> *Eva:* We're just so overwhelmed. It's a long day and you're overwhelmed with clients. They sit at home and they can't wait for Monday morning and they sit out there, sometimes out in

the freezing cold waiting on the clinic to open. I get to work at 7:30, and I'm not lying, clients will be sitting outside wrapped in blankets waiting on the clinic to open, to come in the clinic. I don't understand it. I really don't understand it. And then some come, and I don't know if they use it for their little way of getting out to meet their friends or whatever, a lot of clients will come and spend the day. . . . I don't know what they use the clinic for.
Natalia: Are these clients mostly Latinas and Latinos, or mostly African American or white clients?
Eva: Oh, no, I mean Hispanics. They are the ones who come here, stay all day long, and meet their friends. The other clients come and leave after they're done. (Fieldnotes)

Indeed, many Latina/o clients did meet other Latinas/os at the clinic. Latinas/os would often catch up and talk while waiting to see the clinician or pick up a prescription. The Latina/o clients that "stayed all day long" usually had several appointments at the clinic. It was not unusual for a Latina client to bring two of her children to see a clinician, visit a maternity care coordinator, and pick up formula from the WIC office and medicine from the pharmacy, all in the same day. Many Latina/o clients preferred to do everything in a day, they told me, because child care, transportation to and from the clinic, and taking a day off from work were costly and sometimes impossible.

Many African American staffers thought of Latina/o clients as, in Stephanie's words, "getting something for nothing." In their view, the clinic was, according to Eva, "bending over backwards to serve Hispanics." African Americans' resentment toward Latinas/os was evident when they complained to me that Latinas/os were abusing the system by refusing to learn English and yet still expecting to receive adequate service. For example, Margaret, the clinic receptionist, said the following when I asked her if she had ever thought of learning Spanish:

Margaret: Well I just feel like . . . you know, to me the Hispanics need to learn more English, rather than, you know, I'm expected to learn Spanish, because if they choose to live in a country where obviously the language is different, then I just feel like one should learn it. If I was to go to Europe, or wherever, to live, I need to learn that language. . . . But I have learned certain things, I have. And I think I do, I think I do pretty well as far as making out appointments. But, I will say this, I find if there is no one around me that speaks Spanish, if there is no translator, they can spit out a little English, enough for me to figure out what they need.

Natalia: What do you mean? Can you give me an example?

Margaret: When they're forced to, and the same thing with the telephone. I've learned if there is no one around at all, and sometimes there is no translator, I've learned to say that . . . [the Spanish-speaking receptionist] is at lunch, comiendo. What is it, está comiendo?

Natalia: Está comiendo, yes.

Margaret: Yeah, está comiendo. And they say "okay" and hang up. Or if I say, "Do you speak any English," many say "a little." And I just say "no translator" and then I tell them to explain what they need. And sometimes they can. But I find that if they're forced to, because there's no one around, we can work it out. (Interview)

Margaret implies that Latina/o clients knew at least a bit more English than they let on. This was not the first time I heard the African American staff complain that Latinas/os were not learning English (or pretending not to know). When I was translating for Desiree, the African American lead nurse, she often asked me why "your people" would do things that were "just not right." From my fieldnotes:

Desiree: [O]ne of the greatest complaints I hear is: Why don't Hispanics learn English? It is a two-way thing. I have learned Spanish, well, a little; why don't they learn English? They have children who speak English, they have been here for years, but they don't learn English. . . .

Natalia (purposely not answering the question): Where have you learned Spanish?

Desiree: Here at work. I have learned it here.

Natalia: Have you gone to a class?

Desiree: Oh no. I am too busy with work, church, and family. I have no time. I would feel guilty if I have to leave to go to a class. . .

Desiree implied that she, and by implication other African Americans, would act differently toward Latinas/os if they learned English.

For Desiree, Latinas/os—despite working two or more jobs, working weekdays and weekends, having difficulties with transportation and child care—had no excuse for not learning English. But according to Desiree, it was understandable that she did not learn Spanish; she was overworked and had little free time. In addition, the administrators did not give her time off or pay for her to take Spanish classes. The combination of poor English skills with preconceived notions that Latinas/os are "lazy" and "abusing the system" provide the African American staff at Care Inc. an ideal rationale for attributing a group trait (language skills) to a personal failing (instead of a product of limited time, money, and language classes).

The work was growing more difficult for Care Inc.'s African American lower-status workers because of the changing demographic composition of the clientele (and consequently of the staff), the need for Spanish-language competence to serve the population, and the daily confrontation with a culture with which they were not familiar. It is possible that they also felt less competent to help the clientele, and acquired fewer psychological rewards from helping others and doing a job well, as there was an increasing mismatch between their skills and the needs of the changing population.

However, the African American staff viewed (or discredited) Latinas/os as lazy, working the system, having no regard for rules and discipline, and being bad and irresponsible parents. As a result, African Americans' health-care work was of utmost importance: African American staffers, not Latinas, made Care Inc. what it was and had to keep it afloat by making sure they got their Latina co-workers to do what they were supposed to do; African American staffers, not Latinas, safeguarded the health-care system—and Care Inc. in particular—from the misuse and abuse of some (Latina/o) clients; and finally it was the African American staffers, not Latinas, who were the better mothers and teachers of US morals and values.

African American staff, however, did often defend before family members and friends the right of Latina/o immigrants to have health care, despite the views discussed previously. Importantly, African American staffers defended Latina/o immigrants' right to health care because most of their clientele were now Latinas/os. Perhaps if this population did not require health care their jobs would be even more precarious; thus they defended immigrants' right to affordable medical care. Eva, the African American medical assistant, told me in an interview how she defended "Mexicans'" right to health care before her African American relatives and friends:

> I tell my family, my own family and my friends when they say, "I don't know why you work with them Mexicans." "Excuse me?" I get really upset. I get very angry when I hear that. . . . They say "They're taking over." I said "Who?". . . I mean "Who is 'they'?" And then I have to make them say what they're saying, you know. Don't think it, say it! "You know, those Mexicans are taking over." "No, they're just going looking for care, medical care for themselves. This is where they can get it—so be it. If you want to go somewhere else, so be it. To each his own.

Similarly, when I was observing and translating for the African American triage nurse, Stephanie, she commented after seeing a twenty-four-year-old white woman complaining of a cold: "Some white, even low-income, people come here with such hatred . . . saying 'There are Mexicans everywhere, they are taking over everything, even our clinic.' I identify with the underdog. And they are waiting for me to say 'yes,' but if they think that of Mexicans, they think that of other non-white people, other Hispanics, and of course, African Americans."

For Stephanie it was clear that if this woman was prejudiced against Mexicans, it was very likely that she was prejudiced against all people of color, including African American people. However, when African American staffers or African American clients make these comments, she does not label it as hatred nor does she identify with the Mexicans or Latinas/os.

Lower-Status Latina Staffers

As with the lower-status African American staffers, Latina staffers crafted their moral identity by relying on racial-solidarity rhetoric. They also used class frames. The lower-status Latina health-care practitioners defined Latinos/as as the neediest clients with the fewest resources, who required protection from the "racist" African American staff.

For the lower-status Latina staffers, the difficult working conditions helped them maintain their moral identity, which they crafted by categorizing African American staffers as "racist." As a result, they had to defend Latina/o clients from these African American co-workers. They viewed their health-care work as even more important because, according to Latina staffers, the interests and needs of Latinas/os were not a priority for the clinic, and because the African American staffers "ha[d] the ear of the white administrators and managers," and "the [white] bosses make us bend over backwards so the African Americans feel okay at the clinic, like forc[ing] us not to speak Spanish."

African American Staffers Are "Racists"

Several of the lower-status Latina staffers had been working in the health-care industry for years. However, many had begun work as housekeepers or custodians before they had taken the certified nursing assistant course or the medical assistant (I or II) course and entered the medical field. For example, Tatiana, the Latina receptionist, said in an interview:

> There I worked for two years. Cleaning the apartments when people went away, that were empty. It is hard, but better than cleaning houses. Because I could not stand the backache when I was cleaning houses. But it had to be done, because what else could I do? Working there I saw an opportunity in the newspaper, I saw it, that said that they needed a certain amount of people to take the CNA course, certified nurse's assistant. I always liked nursing. . . . The course lasted a year and three months. I received my certification from the state as a nurse's assistant. Then I started working only as a nurse assistant.

> Allí trabajé como por dos años. Limpiando los apartamentos que se iba la gente, que ya quedaba vacíos. Está, estaba duro, pero mejor que limpiar cuartos. Porque yo no aguantaba la espalda limpiando cuartos. Pero tenía que hacer, porque ¿qué más? Trabajando allí salió una oportunidad en el periódico, yo la vi, que decía que necesitaba cierta cantidad de personas para

tomar el curso de CNA, certified nurse's assistant. Entonces a mí siempre me gustaba la enfermería. . . . El curso duró un año tres meses. Saqué mi certificación del estado de nurse's assistant. Entonces ya me dediqué a trabajar solo de asistente de enfermera.

Similarly, Amanda, a Latina client-care coordinator, recalled why she began working in the medical industry after cleaning houses for several years: "I wanted to get into a medical field or anything, anything to do with patients."

As described before, at Care Inc., the Latina and African American staff occupied lower-status positions; however, because of seniority, African American staffers trained and supervised Latina staffers. The Latina staff disliked this, as Amanda explained during a break:

> You know, like, what we're finding out lately, me and Tatiana [the Latina receptionist], is that, like the lady in the back [Diane, an African American woman in charge of medical records], obviously she's got way too much time on her hands, because she's constantly watching who's coming in, you know, who's leaving at what time. That's not her job. Like, you know, she's got her job. Her job isn't like the supervisor, where she's checking employees about who comes and who doesn't come and who stays and all this other stuff. So Margaret [the African American receptionist] and her get together on this. And then they go ahead and call corporate, you know, call corporate to say, "Well, you know, this person didn't come," or "Where is she?" (Fieldnotes)

The Latina staff assumed that the African American staff had more power and advantages than the Latina staff. The Latina staff criticized the African American staff for being authoritarian and making more work for them by asking them to translate. Latina staffers also argued that administrators cared more about African American staffers' needs, and that African American clients had other options for jobs, health care, and other social services that Latina/o clients lacked because they were not US citizens. As a result, the Latina staff claimed that African American women were more powerful both inside and outside of Care Inc.

At the clinic, all the white staff members spoke Spanish or were learning to speak Spanish. The only staff members who did not speak Spanish were African American: Stephanie (the triage nurse), Desiree (the lead nurse), Margaret (the receptionist), Diane and Penny (the two African American women in charge of medical records), and Eva and Genesis (the two African American medical assistants). The only African American on staff who spoke Spanish was Dr. Sikes, who left the clinic to work in private practice in December 2003. The African American staff members were encouraged to take Spanish classes, but the administrators did not offer them time off to learn Spanish or reimbursement for classes. The white staff, on the other hand, had learned Spanish either during college or by taking an immersion and intensive Spanish course in a Central American country (at a personal expense of over $1,000 per week), which was often done during vacation time.

The Latinas did not recognize the systemic inequality the African American female staff (or African Americans in general) experienced on a daily basis. Instead, they questioned claims that the African American women were victims of racism because the Latina staff felt these African American women were "racist" themselves.

All the Latina staff members I talked to said that the African American staffers were "racist." The Latina staff complained that they were victims of discrimination or, at the very least, were mistreated by the African American staff. Carlotta, the recently hired assistant maternity care coordinator, said in an interview how she had already heard disparaging comments from Stanley, the African American male working in WIC: "que nosotros los hispanos llegamos a este país a quitarle el trabajo a ellos los negros." ["That we, Latinos, arrived in this country to take away the jobs of them, the African Americans."]

Barbara and Bibiana, the Latina medical assistants, often complained to each other (and to me) about the "racist comments" made by the African American medical assistants and nurses. For example, Barbara complained about Stephanie, the African American triage nurse, and Eva, an African American medical assistant, after her African American co-workers chastised Latina clients for abusing the US health-care system by coming to the clinic "too often." From my fieldnotes: "Stephanie, who came into the nurses' station, said to Eva: 'People can't be that sick.' Eva replied: 'I know what you mean. . . . See that woman (Latina) with that plastic bag from Wal-Mart? She came in yesterday. I can't believe it. Why would they [the Latina and her son] bring that big plastic Spiderman balloon with them? Certain things are left at home.' Stephanie said, 'Don't they have anything better to do? We're not giving anything away here. Argh, these people!'"

Bibiana, standing by the nurses' station entrance door, then said: "They [Stephanie and Eva] are just ignorant and disrespectful people. Don't all people have the right to come to the clinic as many times as they feel they need to get medical care?" Barbara nodded in agreement.

I observed instances in which Latina staff characterized African American staff's interaction with Latina/o clients as mistreatment: "Trish, the white woman in charge of billing, is at lunch and it is time for Tatiana, the Latina receptionist, to go home. Tatiana asks Diane, the African American woman in charge of medical records: 'Diane, you know, I don't think Trish's coming back. Do you mind just staying on the window for an hour?' Diane agreed. When a Latina client asked Diane for something, she said: 'I don't want to hear it!'" (Fieldnotes).

Amanda, a Latina patient-care coordinator, observed Diane's interaction with the Latina client. Amanda said to me:

> Well, Diane had to fuss over it. Like, if Tatiana would have asked me, I would have gladly said, "No problem. . . . Do what you have to do." But when she [Diane] doesn't want to do it, she makes a fuss. She's racist, and she takes it out on the [Latina/o] clients. Her hands were going, and she was like, "I don't want to hear it!" The [Latina] client was just asking a question. But because she didn't want to be in the window, she took it out on the client. The client had nothing to do with it. (Fieldnotes)

On another occasion Tatiana, a Latina receptionist, complained to me about Margaret, an African American:

> *Tatiana:* It makes me so upset and sad to see how Margaret treats the Hispanic clients.
> *Natalia:* How does Margaret treat the clients?

Tatiana: She treats them badly. She is a racist. She is always saying to them, "No English? Can't help you."

Tatiana: Me da rabia y lástima cómo Margaret trata a los pacientes hispanos.
Natalia: ¿Cómo trata Margaret a los pacientes?
Tatiana: Ella los trata mal. Es racista. Siempre les está diciendo, "No English? Can't help you." (Fieldnotes)

Some of the African American staff did not understand the Latina staff's complaints about them. Latina staffers did not complain directly to the African American staff, but to the white higher-status staff, who then talked to the African American staff. After some Latina staffers complained about Stephanie, she responded by saying to me, "I am black, so how can I be racist? I have lived all my life with racism, and I would never be racist!"

On one level, Stephanie was right. Racism in the United States is a system that privileges whites over people of color (Mills 1997; Omi and Winant 1994; Tatum 2003; Wellman 1993). A white person who is not racist still has advantages in a racist society; she or he has unearned white advantages (Carbado 1999; McIntosh 1997). Some sociologists define racism as prejudice plus power: "[R]acial prejudice when combined with social power—access to social, cultural, and economic resources and decision-making—leads to the institutionalization of racist policies and practices" (Tatum 2003, 7–8). By these definitions of racism, African Americans, as members of an oppressed group, have little power to enforce their prejudices and thus cannot be racist. As a social system, racism requires the power to enforce discrimination and prejudice against others. And yet, by accusing the African American staff of being racist, the Latinas dismissed any notion that these African American women might also be victims.

On another level, however, African Americans (like whites) can be prejudiced and maintain that Latinas/os and other immigrant groups are inferior. If they act on these prejudices, African Americans (like whites) can discriminate against immigrants. Latinas/os are often targeted because they are not US citizens. Latina/o immigrants are denied medical care and social services on a daily basis. Many US citizens don't have health insurance, either, but they are not always denied access to health care because they are US citizens. They might be denied medical care because they are women, poor, African American, or members of other oppressed groups in the United States (US Department of Health and Human Services 2005). As with other immigrants, Latina/o immigrants are denied health-care services, along with other social services, simply because they are immigrants. As federal, state, and local funds shrank and the number of uninsured grew due to the 2009–10 recession and immigration pressure, health officials cut non-emergency health services for undocumented immigrants all over the United States. This meant that non-emergency health services were cut for approximately 59 percent of the 11.9 million undocumented immigrants living in the United States who have no health insurance, or about 15 percent of the nation's approximately 47 million uninsured.

At Care Inc., the African American staffers did not recognize their citizenship privilege (Schwalbe 2002), and the Latina staff minimized the way white racism in the United States shaped the African American staff's lives. For example, Latina staff resented the fact that they were not allowed to bring their young children to work on Monday afternoons and evenings, when they had to work until 8 p.m. As Carlotta, the recently hired assistant maternity care coordinator, explained in an interview:

> It is discrimination that the children of staff cannot come to the clinic nor stay at the clinic on Mondays when we have to stay here until eight at night. One cannot leave a twelve- or thirteen-year-old son alone at home. The police will arrive because you are a terrible mother, a child abuser. And you will have to leave them alone because you do not have your father, your mother, your grandmother, your granddaughter, your cousin, or your niece to help you take care of your son. The only option is taking him to the office. But here you can't. These are the small details.

> Es una discriminacion que los hijos de los empleados no puedan venir a la clínica ni quedarse en la clínica los lunes cuando nos tenemos que quedar aquí hasta las ocho de la noche. Uno no va a dejar a su hijo de doce o trece sólo en la casa. Te llega la policía porque eres una coñá madre, eres una child abuser. Y te

toca dejarlos solos porque no tienes a tu papá, a tu mamá, a tu abuela, a tu nieta, a tu prima, o a tu sobrina que te cuiden tu hijo. Tu única opción, llevarlo para la oficina. Entones aquí no. Estos son los detallitos.

As a result, both groups exaggerated the other group's privileges. As we will see, this exaggeration of differences was made easier by prevailing stereotypes of African American women as argumentative and aggressive.

The lower-status Latina workers' master narrative about their moral selves categorized Latinas/os as the moral, "needy" clients, themselves as the "moral" health-care workers, and African American women as "racist." As in the case of the lower-status African American staff, their crafting of a moral identity relied on racial-solidarity rhetoric. Their moral identity was also crafted by using class frames and nationalist frames: they defined Latinos/as as needy, having few resources and health-care options, and discriminated against by North Carolinians—in particular, by African Americans.

5

"Neediest of the Needy"

How Midlevel-Status Workers
View Their Work as "Moral" *

THE MATERNITY CARE COORDINATORS provided family planning and contraceptive counseling for all women who came to Care Inc. for a free pregnancy test. They saw all new prenatal clients before their first visit with a clinician. In this one-hour visit, the maternity care coordinators provided clients with information about Care Inc.'s services, the WIC nutrition program, and North Carolina's Baby Love program. They also took applications for Pregnant Women's Medicaid program and Infants' and Children's Medicaid program. Medicaid is an assistance program that provides medical and health-related services for low-income families, a jointly funded cooperative venture that began in 1965 between the federal and state governments to assist states in providing medical care to eligible needy persons (see: http://cms.hhs.gov/medicaid/mover.asp). In this first visit, and in subsequent prenatal visits, the maternity care coordinators evaluated the women's pregnancy-related needs and recommended services or plans to meet those needs. The maternity care coordinators were also trained to intervene in cases where they suspected a woman was being abused by her partner or when a child was being mistreated or abused.

*A condensed version of this analysis was published in 2007: "Helping the 'Neediest of the Needy': An Intersectional Analysis of Moral-Identity Construction at a Community Health Clinic," *Gender & Society* 21(5):749–772.

The maternity care coordinators taught a six-week birthing class for Latinas in their second or third trimester of pregnancy. This program was implemented in 1988 when Care Inc. became one of the 206 federally funded community centers to which the US Congress gave money "to implement services to improve pregnancy outcomes and reduce infant death rates" (*History and introduction to [Care Inc.] perinatal program*). When the clinic first opened in 1970, 80 percent of the clients were African American. By 2002, 57 percent of the clients were Latinas and Latinos, 17 percent were white, and 16 percent were African American. Only a year later the proportion of Latina and Latino clients had increased by 10 percent. Since 1990, some Southern states, including North Carolina, have become common destinations for Latina/o immigrants. According to the US Census Bureau, North Carolina's Latina/o population has grown 394 percent since 1990, and Latinas/os account for 4.7 percent of the state's population. The rapid growth of the state's Latina/o population outpaced the nationwide rate of almost 60 percent since 1990 (US Census Bureau 2010).

The maternity care coordinators also dealt with difficult working conditions. They were poorly paid, overworked, and interacted with clients experiencing physical and economic hardships. Despite these challenges, they constructed a positive self-image, a moral identity (Kleinman 1996) that helped them persevere under difficult circumstances. These maternity care coordinators, two of them white and two of them Latina, saw themselves not only as good people, but also as health practitioners responsible for helping the "neediest of the needy" (as one maternity care coordinator put it). The maternity care coordinators' moral identity relied upon characterizing the Latinas as the "moral" clients, while demonizing the attitude of African American Care Inc. staffers.

The maternity care coordinators identified Latinas as those who needed them the most, and they became allies for these Latinas. In doing so, they lumped the other clients—African American and white women—into the category they called "American." The term "American" became a synonym for privilege, at least relative to Latinas. The white and Latina maternity care coordinators felt they needed to protect and save Latina clients from the discrimination they experienced in wider society and, as the maternity care coordinators' saw it, from the African American staff of Care Inc. as well.

It is not surprising for US citizens to refer to themselves as "Americans." In the broadest use, the term includes any US citizen, regardless of her or his ethnicity, race, sex, class, or sexual orientation. So how did it come to be used differently by the maternity care coordinators? They used the term descriptively, but also at times in a way that was synonymous with privilege. For example, Melanie, a white maternity care coordinator, used it in an interview to describe her family: "My dad is American. My dad is as white as you can be—born and raised in southern California. My mother was born in the Philippines. . . . Her mother was half-Spanish and half-American." Melanie used the term to describe her "American" clients as compared to her "Latina" clients:

> I think with my Latina clients that I work with that they expect a more personal relationship. . . . The first month I was working at the clinic, every time I meet a new woman they always asked me: Do you have children? Are you married? You know, do you have a boyfriend? Why don't you have a boyfriend? (Laughing) Where's your family? They want to develop this personal relationship. . . . The sort of interaction that I have is different to the one I have with my American clients, because they're more used to a professional relationship. There is this black line that you don't cross it when you're talking with any professional, you know, your maternity care coordinator or your physician or your social worker. With my Latina clients, it's just, it's just different. (Interview)

The maternity care coordinators, however, also used the term "Americans" at times to refer to the African American clients who made their work difficult. When I probed them for what they meant by "Americans," the maternity care coordinators replied that they meant African American women. For example, when I asked Yolanda, a Latina maternity care coordinator, about her clients, she said in an interview:

> Racism is horrible from Americans, from blacks. It is incredible! Now, as this is a different position, because supposedly the

MCCs are more respected, I feel it less. But that does not mean that I do not identify with my fellow Hispanic staff members. I feel it as if they were doing it to me.

El racismo es horrible de parte de los americanos, de los negros. Es increíble! Ahora, como ésta es una posición distinta, pues supuestamente las MCC las respetan más, yo lo siento menos. Pero eso no quiere decir que yo no me siento identificada con mis compañeras que son hispanas también. Lo siento como que me lo estuvieran haciendo a mí.

The other maternity care coordinators echoed Yolanda's assessment of African American patients. They commented about "difficult" people by referring to them as "American." When I asked them to clarify what they meant by "Americans" they explained that these clients were African American women. By using "American" instead of black, they avoided a racial discussion and focused instead on the lack of privileges experienced by Latinas. Using the term also enabled the white maternity care coordinators to build solidarity with their Latina counterparts without appearing racially insensitive to other African American staff at the clinic. All maternity care coordinators felt Latina clients were especially "needy" and deserving of special protection; guarding over them was a crucial component of their moral identity.

My observations and analysis center on three of the clinic's four maternity care coordinators. Because Rachel, the supervisor of the maternity care coordinators and a maternity care coordinator herself, spent most of her time writing grants and doing administrative work during my time at Care Inc., I rarely observed her interacting with other maternity care coordinators or clients. Rachel was white, a US citizen, and the only maternity care coordinator not fluent in Spanish. She interacted only with English-speaking clients (white, black, or Latina). She had worked at Care Inc. for more than four years and oversaw the work done by the other three maternity care coordinators.

Melanie, the youngest maternity care coordinator, was a twenty-five-year-old white US citizen. She started working at Care Inc. in 2001 after receiving a master's degree in public health. She left Care Inc. in December 2002 to study medicine at a university on the West Coast. She was replaced four months later by another young white

US citizen who worked for only a few months before quitting; when I finished my observations, she had not been replaced. Yolanda, a Latina in her late thirties, came to the United States seven years earlier from her native Venezuela. Yolanda had been working at Care Inc. for more than five years, the longest of the three maternity care coordinators. Yolanda quit her job and left for a higher paying one in March 2003. MariaTe, also Latina, was in her early thirties and came from Mexico in 2000. Both Yolanda and MariaTe had US green cards. Although MariaTe's official job title was that of a maternity care coordinator assistant, she did almost the same work as the other maternity care coordinators. Melanie often pointed this out: "MariaTe does the same work I do, without the respect, the salary, or the title we have. I wish she could apply for my job, but this is a sore subject" (Fieldnotes).

The MCCs did recognize the demands put on Rachel in her supervisory position. For example, Melanie, when complaining about a client she had just counseled, said: "Rachel usually sees the American women. But like she is not here, we have to do it. I don't know what is going on with her. She is always writing her grants, and she doesn't chip in. But nothing!" (Fieldnotes). Similarly, when MariaTe and Melanie complained about Rachel, they said: "If she only opened her door, she would know what we do!. . . Or if she were here" (Fieldnotes).

Maternity care coordinators devised three strategies to feel good about themselves as health providers: defining maternal health as a feminist mission; defending clients from (African American) staff; and categorizing clients as either "Americans" or "Latinas."

Maternal Care as a Feminist Mission

The first strategy used by Care Inc.'s maternity care coordinators to enhance their moral identity was to define maternal-care work as part of a feminist mission. For example, the maternity care coordinators often commented on how their services "improved women's, infants', and families' health and well-being" (Fieldnotes). The maternity care coordinators emphasized their good intentions for doing maternal-care work by invoking the importance of empowering women. Even if they perceived non-Latina clients as having more options, they were still women. As Rachel explained to me: "Our job is to educate and to provide the best service and care we can to those we can serve. We empower" (Fieldnotes).

Melanie also viewed her job as giving power to women by educating them. When I asked her to describe her work, she said:

> Pregnancy tests take up a lot of time, but they're actually one of my favorite things about my job. I think that when you do a pregnancy test it's what we call the teachable moment. It's just a really good opportunity to do good reproductive-health counseling. Women are normally pretty receptive, and so I can do a lot of talking and teaching about contraceptive options. Even when doing options counseling to someone that is pregnant and is not sure if they want to keep the baby or not, which can be stressful, I enjoy talking to the women and helping them to think out their decisions, and helping them think about what they want to do and what the next step is going to be. For me, that's just something that I really like. (Interview)

An important part of the maternity care coordinators' work was to clarify a woman's options: continuing the pregnancy, putting the newborn up for adoption, or obtaining an abortion. The maternity care coordinators said that giving women knowledge about all the choices available to them granted the women "freedom," "control," and "power." They constantly cited the help they offered women under difficult circumstances as evidence that their work was more than a job: it was a mission. Rachel emphasized the importance of offering abortion as an option to women:

> My view on abortion is very clear. Abortion is a way for women to have control over reproduction. Some women might use it as a method of birth control. For others it is what they do as their last resort. And others do it when there is a problem with the fetus, when there is a disability, or when the fetus dies. Abortion is about control. Abortion is a choice. I believe that women must have the choice to have an abortion, and therefore women must have knowledge about it. Knowledge is power; knowledge is liberty. (Fieldnotes)

MariaTe also thought of maternal-care work as a mission. She said:

> If there is someone with a positive pregnancy test, and she does not want the baby, then you are there to help her, to support her in what she wants, in what she decides, without judging her. That's the best. It's the opportunity that someone is there with her while she decides to abort or not. I never imagined how important this help is. For example, I had the case of a teen that wanted to abort and did not have the money. I think it is great that I am able to tell her: OK, we will do things to help you get the money for this.

> Si hay alguien que tiene una prueba de embarazo positiva y no quiere al bebé, que tú estés allí para ayudarla, apoyarla en lo que ella quiera, en lo que ella decida, sin juzgarla es lo mejor. Es el hecho de que haya alguien que esté allí, con ella, mientras ella toma la decisión de aborto o no aborto. Nunca me imaginé que pudiera ayudar tanto y que fuera tan necesaria esa ayuda. Por ejemplo, tuve el caso de una chavita que quería abortar y no tenía dinero. Se me hace padre poderle decir: bueno, podremos mover cosas para que consigas este dinero para esto. (Interview)

And Melanie said: "I consider my work feminist work. I think feminism is helping women achieve what they want to achieve in life. Helping them meet goals and set goals and be able to make changes in their lives depending on what they want. And I do that."

She recognized the importance of giving information as "planting a seed," especially for Latinas:

> I have some clients who have had four babies and want to have a fifth because they must have a son. I don't agree with it. Why do they need to have the son? They don't. But how can I convince her she doesn't need a son? It is not my place to tell her that. It's not my place to tell her what to do. I can only provide to her new information, plant a seed, and get her to think about things. And the truth is that most of the time women choose to do things I—as a feminist—disagree with. And there is not

much I can do. I can only give her all the information I have for her to make an informed decision. (Interview)

Yet for the maternity care coordinators, defining their work as feminist was double-edged; it became a source of frustration as well as value. As Melanie said: "Most of the time women choose to do things I—as a feminist—disagree with." Rachel, who also defined herself and her work as feminist, described the difficulties of empowering women while not creating dependence:

It's a real fine line for the staff here to provide services and assistance without creating dependence. How do you empower somebody when the agency doesn't even speak the same language? And there are so many needs and issues, basic needs like food, clothing, and shelter. How do you get past that point of meeting those basic needs to say: "You need to speak out, and you need to be political; these are services that you have a right to, that you should have a right to, you have the right to fight against discrimination!" So it's hard, I think, for the staff, because the need is so great. We can't be everything to everybody, and if we try to be, we burn out; if we try to be [everything to everybody] also we're enabling. It's hard to know where to define that line. . . . I think, sometimes, by making a lot of noise you can bring about change, but sometimes you need to back off. (Interview)

"Dependent" clients were a threat to their moral identity because they exhibited more than just "need." Dependent clients can expect too much of the maternity care coordinators and prevent them from helping those who are willing to help themselves. When maternity care coordinators sensed dependence, they felt justified in "back[ing] off."

As long as the maternity care coordinators did not sense dependence, they saw themselves as advocates not only for clients, but also for women in general. MariaTe also defined her work, in particular the education she provided, as feminist. When I interviewed her she said:

I feel like a feminist because I believe that gender roles are distributed very badly and because I believe that the woman is subordinate. Something that infuriates me and I cannot support is a woman being subservient to a man or her male children, or her children in general, male or female. I feel that I can deliver an attack to break those gender schemes. I feel that, in that sense of my work, I have the opportunity to do those things because I tell women you do not have to do this, and you do not have to have children today, you do not have to stay in your house to work, that your husband does not have the right to decide your life. I feel that in that sense, my work gives me the opportunity to send those messages, and if one out of ten gets it, I did it.

Yo me siento como feminista porque sí creo que los roles del género están muy mal distribuídos y porque creo que la mujer está rezagada. Algo que me emputa y no lo puedo soportar es a una mujer sirviéndole a un hombre o a sus hijos hombres, a sus hijos en general hombres y mujeres. Siento que hago un esfuerzo por romper esos esquemas. Siento que en ese sentido de mi trabajo tengo oportunidad de hacer esas cosas porque cada que puedo trato de abrir luces de que no tienes que hacer esto, y no tienes que tener hijos hoy, no tienes que quedarte en tu casa a trabajar, que tu esposo no tiene por qué decidir tu vida. Siento que en ese sentido mi trabajo me da oportunidad de mandar esos mensajes y que si pegan en una de diez ya la hice.

Later in the interview, MariaTe recognized the importance of doing feminist work with Latinas. She said:

In the prenatal classes [only for Latinas] I have the opportunity to repeat the message, repeat the message, repeat the message. In the classes I tell them: You do not have to stay in your house to work and your husband does not have the right to decide your life.

En las clases prenatales [solo para Latinas] constantemente tengo la oportunidad de estar repitiendo el mensaje, repitiendo el mensaje, repitiendo el mensaje. En las clases les digo: no tienes que quedarte en tu casa a trabajar y que tu esposo no tiene por qué decidir tu vida.

The maternity care coordinators recognized the difficulties of doing maternity care at Care Inc. and often saw their work as a Band-Aid, not a cure. They did not see their work as capable of ending gender inequality, but as a positive force in a long struggle. The distance separating their current position and their ultimate goal actually helped them maintain their moral identity. Without a struggle, their mission became merely a job. The ideology and rhetoric of the feminist movement was an important tool to maintain a sense of themselves as good people.

Defending Latina Patients against the African American Staff

The maternity care coordinators maintained that they had to defend Latina clients against prejudiced African American staffers at the clinic outside of the maternity care coordinator unit. In addition, Latina staffers complained about the "bad environment" and the negative remarks they heard from African American clients and the African American staff about Latinas/os (both staff and clients). I observed African American staffers complaining often about the Latina/o clients and Latina staff. For example, some African American staffers told me in interviews that the source of difficulties at work was the Latina staff: "staff have not been able—or willing as some are saying—to get the job done"; staff "form racial cliques and are against the other people." The lower-status workers, African Americans and Latinas, formed racially divided groups that prioritized their own racial group interests.

The African American staff members' attitude might well have been their response to the rapid change in clientele at Care Inc. In 1970, when the clinic opened, it served African American community members almost exclusively. By 2000, however, it had come to serve mostly Latinas/os. The African American staff felt that the clinic was replacing the needs of the surrounding African American community with the needs of Latinas/os. This sentiment is evident in the comments several African American staff said to me and to other staffers: "Hispanics are now getting everything we blacks fought years for," and "Hispanics are taking over our clinic."

Although these demographic changes within the community were beyond the control of the staff at Care Inc., they affected the way the staff viewed their actions. Insensitive treatment could be interpreted as defending one's group interests. Privileging one group of clients over another could be seen as defending them against unjust attacks. All of these actions had to be negotiated within a moral identity that justified the actions as fair.

The maternity care coordinators complained about the malicious comments about Latina clients they heard from African American staff, and they claimed that they needed to protect Latina clients from them. For example, MariaTe acknowledged that she spent a lot of time "defending and protecting" Latinas/os. I recorded the following conversation between MariaTe and Melanie:

> *MariaTe:* It's incredible, but approximately 50 percent of my job is defending Hispanics. We have to protect ourselves. The blacks defend blacks, and Hispanics defend Hispanics. And I tell you that the blacks protect blacks, so we [Hispanics] have to unite ourselves in the fights.
> *Melanie:* I know. I also spend my time helping my Hispanic women.

> *MariaTe:* Es increíble, pero aproximadamente 50 por ciento de mi trabajo es defiendo a hispanos. Toca protegernos. Los negros defienden a los negros, y los hispanos defienden a los hispanos. Y te digo los negros protegen a los negros, entonces nosotros [hispanos] tenemos que unirnos en las broncas.
> *Melanie:* Lo sé. Yo me la paso también ayudando a mis hispanas.

The Latina maternity care coordinators saw themselves as more than just health practitioners; they were spokespeople assigned the duty of protecting the reputation of their community (and, by extension, themselves). By complaining to Melanie, MariaTe was also seeking out solidarity between white and Latina staff. Latina clients also felt comfortable complaining to both white and Latina staff about the tone, comments, treatment, and/or service they received from "las morenas" (African American female staff). Latina/o clients claimed that they were mistreated by the African American staff. When I asked the maternity care coordinators to describe some of the clients' complaints, they recalled: "Son tan bruscas [they are so rough]"; "Me tratan peor que un animal, como si no fuera un humano [They treat me worse than an animal, as if I were not human]"; and "No nos quieren aquí, y no les importa lo que nos pasa o le pasa a mis hijos [They do not want us here, and they do not care what happens to us or to my children]." These confidential complaints were interpreted as proof by the maternity care coordinators that they needed to look out for each other and protect Latina clients if need be.

Latina and white maternity care coordinators said they frequently overheard African American staffers and African American clients make snide remarks about Latinas. They complained to each other (and to me) about some of the following comments allegedly made by African American staffers: "Another pregnant woman? They breed like bunnies!" or "The first thing they [Latinas] do when they get here is get pregnant. They do it for citizenship." These comments gave the maternity care coordinators yet another reason to feel protective of the Latina clients. The racialized tensions at the clinic reinforced the maternity care coordinators' focus on Latinas as the neediest and themselves as their protectors. MariaTe and Yolanda often commented on how they, too, had been victims of discrimination by African Americans:

> *MariaTe:* [B]efore, it was difficult to get a driver's license. Now it is impossible for Hispanics. The first time I went to get my driver's license I did not pass the driving exam. I had to take the exam again because I made one mistake. Only one! I drove perfectly for 15 minutes!
> *Yolanda:* My experience was worse. I tried to get a driver's license in Atlanta. An African American woman asked me "Do you know English?" I said, "Not much." And she said, "Come back when you know English." I swear, that is what she said. They are shit.

> *MariaTe:* [A]ntes era difícil pedir una licencia de conducir. Ahora es imposible para hispanos. La primera vez que fui a sacarla no me pasaron. Me tocó tomar el examen de nuevo porque cometí un error. ¡Solo uno! ¡Manejé perfecto por 15 minutos!

Yolanda: Para mí fue peor. Yo lo traté de sacar en Atlanta. La morena me preguntó, "¿Sabe inglés?" Le dije, "No mucho." Y me dijo, "Vuelva cuando sepa inglés." Se los juro, eso me dijo. Son la mierda. (Fieldnotes)

By using "defensive othering" (Schwalbe et al. 2000)—the process by which one "othered" group (in this case, Latinas) constructs boundaries between themselves and other stigmatized groups (in this case, African American staff) while at the same time defining themselves as morally superior to them—the Latina maternity care coordinators defined Latinas as good or valued. The more difficult the maternity care coordinators' work, the greater sense of importance they attached to it.

Difficult "Americans" and Sweet Latinas

The final strategy—categorizing clients as either "Americans" or "Latinas"—drew on racial frames and class frames. The maternity care coordinators identified Latinas as those who needed them the most and became allies for them. In doing so, they lumped all the other clients—African American and white women—into the category they called "American." The term "American" became a synonym for privilege, at least relative to Latinas; the maternity care coordinators' narrative about the moral client defined Latinas as "sweet," as well as being the neediest and having the fewest resources.

Although African American and white clients only occasionally behaved with an "attitude" toward the three maternity care coordinators, these incidents made a strong impression on the maternity care coordinators. In the five months I did fieldwork at the maternity care coordinator unit, the three maternity care coordinators saw few African American and white women. A couple of these African American clients at the clinic expressed defiance or resentment toward the maternity care coordinators, especially the Latina maternity care coordinators. I recorded this interaction in my fieldnotes:

An African American woman, in her mid- or late thirties, was waiting to talk with Yolanda. Yolanda had her door closed as she was counseling a Latina. The African American woman paced outside Yolanda's door and said out loud: "This is ridiculous, I have been waiting here for more than thirty minutes. I have things to do. I can't be here all day like others." MariaTe, after counseling a Latina, asked the African American client: "Can I help you?" The woman replied: "What?" MariaTe repeated her question: "Yolanda is busy, can I help you?" The woman said, raising her voice and talking slowly: "I guess you will do."

This African American client complained that Latina clients "stayed all day long" at the clinic, a luxury she could not afford. It is true that many Latina clients preferred to do everything in a day. Latina clients told me that they would schedule most of their appointments on one day because child care, transportation to and from the clinic, and taking a day off from work were costly and sometimes impossible. On the other hand, African American clients could not wait all day at the clinic as many had to get back to work, or had children at home, or had other responsibilities and errands to run.

After counseling this client, MariaTe said to me, "They talk to me as if I were a retard." During my observations of the maternity care coordinators, MariaTe asked me on five occasions to take a call from an "American" client she could not understand and who was "being rude." MariaTe and Yolanda often asked Melanie or Rachel to handle a client who was making them feel incompetent. The white maternity care coordinators came to the aid of the Latina maternity care coordinators, saying how "unfair" the client was, how "sorry" they were, and that they would "deal with the problem."

The African American clients' attitude might well have been a response to racism against African Americans outside the clinic (Feagin and McKinney 2002). It might also have been a response to the rapid change in the demographics of the clients served by Care Inc. African American clients might have felt that the clinic was replacing their needs with the needs of Latinas. When a few African American clients gave the maternity care coordinators "a piece of their mind," "told them off," or demanded services, it might have been a way for these African American women to assert a sense of control, dignity, and self-respect in the face of systematic inequality and discrimination. These interactions with African American clients also served a dual purpose for the maternity care coordinators: it made their work environment more challenging (and thus more important) and provided an opportunity to come to the protection of their Latina clients.

The maternity care coordinators reported that their difficult clients were African American women whom they categorized as "Americans." The maternity care coordinators complained about women who were not grateful for their help. Melanie, after giving the results of a pregnancy test to an African American client, said to MariaTe:

> She was rude and demanding. Of course, she had to be an American. Nine out of ten times, the problem is the Americans. In the year I have been working here, I swear, she is the rudest. The Hispanics are caring, they are more like my friends.

> Fue muy descortés y demandante. Claro, tenía que ser americana. Nueve de diez veces, el problema son las americanas. En un año que trabajo aquí, lo juro, es la más descortés. Las hispanas son cariñosas; son más como mis amigas. (Fieldnotes)

Melanie said: "I work with an American population who tends to be problematic." Melanie was put off by clients whom she saw as not having a legitimate need for the services of Care Inc.

For the Latina maternity care coordinators, the clients who made them feel incompetent were "Americans" whom they labeled "difficult." After counseling an African American client, Yolanda said to MariaTe and to me:

> I hope they hire another MCC soon. You know, the Americans talk to me in a tone, as if they were telling me, "Yes, you are stupid." And they get upset when I do not understand all that they say and I ask them to repeat it.

> Espero que contraten a otra MCC pronto. Saben, las americanas me hablan con un tonito, es como diciéndome, "Sí, tú eres una pendeja." Y se ponen bravas cuando no les entiendo lo que dicen y les pido que repitan. (Fieldnotes)

When I asked Yolanda, "What has been your experience with clients at the clinic?" she replied:

> *Yolanda:* Black women are demanding. White people are not. White people are educated, the majority. Black women expect a lot of me and are rude. Not all, of course, but most of the black women.
> *Natalia:* And the white women are not like this?
> *Yolanda:* No. White women are more educated. Black women don't say "please" or "thanks."

> *Yolanda:* Las morenas son demandantes. La gente blanca no lo es. La gente blanca es educada, la mayoría. Las morenas esperan mucho de uno y además son groseras. Claro que no todas, pero sí la mayoría de morenas.
> *Natalia:* ¿Y las blancas no son así?
> *Yolanda:* No. La gente blanca es más educada. Las morenas nunca dicen "por favor" o "gracias." (Fieldnotes)

The three maternity care coordinators asserted that they preferred Latina clients. Latinas' gratitude to the maternity care coordinators made it easier for the maternity care coordinators to see themselves as good health-care providers (and as helping those truly in need). The interactions I observed between the maternity care coordinators and the Latinas were relaxed and informal. At a maternity care coordinator staff meeting, Yolanda, Melanie, and MariaTe were talking about Doña Rosario, a 45-year-old woman, who had recently given birth:

> *Melanie:* I just saw Doña Rosario. Her baby is so pretty. And she is so sweet. She is one of my favorite clients.
> *MariaTe:* She is one of my favorites, too.
> *Melanie:* She is 45 years old and just had a baby. It was an accident of menopause. When she learned she was pregnant, she did not tell her family because she was embarrassed. She only told them when she was six months pregnant. But they help her so much. She is always with a family member, and they love her a lot. She has four other children.

Yolanda: Yes, she is from Michoacán. She is so sweet!

MariaTe: And the baby is precious. Doña Rosario always asks, "What do you think of her? Pretty, eh?"

Melanie: Acabo de ver a Doña Rosario. La bebé está tan bonita. Y ella es tan dulce. Ella es una de mis pacientes favoritas.

MariaTe: Ella es una de las mías también.

Melanie: Ella tiene 45 años y acaba de tener una bebé. Fue un accidente de menopausia. Ella cuando supo [que estaba embarazada] no le dijo a nadie de su familia, por pena. Ella estaba apenada. Solo les dijo a los seis meses. Pero la ayudan tanto. Siempre está acompañada, y la quieren mucho. Ella tiene 4 hijos más.

Yolanda: Sí, es de Michoacán. ¡Es tan dulce!

MariaTe: Y la bebé es preciosa. Doña Rosario siempre me pregunta, "¡¿Cómo la ves, bonita, eh?!" (Fieldnotes)

The maternity care coordinators might not have seen this woman, a person under their care who had an unwanted pregnancy, as an ideal client. Or, they might have seen this woman as having initiated prenatal care very late. Instead, Doña Rosario was their favorite. But consider how they reacted to an African American teen who came in for a pregnancy test, even though she was taking birth control pills and had used condoms during sex. Melanie brought up this patient as an example of someone who was "difficult":

Melanie: I have this one woman, who, she comes in to do a pregnancy test every two weeks, and I just think she does it 'cause she likes to touch base. I mean, she's taking birth control pills and using condoms. I mean, there's like no chance in the world that, that she is going to get pregnant, but, she just needs someone to touch base with. She came in when she got engaged and showed me her engagement ring and, that's kind of all done on the guise of pregnancy testing. But, she pretty much knows she's not pregnant.

Natalia: Is she Latina?

Melanie: Oh no, she is an African American teenager. Americans are the difficult ones. (Fieldnotes)

Melanie might have seen this woman as an ideal client, a person under her care who was doing things right. Or, she might have seen this teenager as lonely and in need of care. Instead, she saw this client as wasting her time. Prioritizing Latina clients' needs did not threaten Melanie's moral identity; instead, it bolstered it (because Latina clients do not waste limited time and resources just to "touch base").

The maternity care coordinators thought of Latinas as grateful and respectful. When Latina clients did not act this way, the maternity care coordinators described them as behaving "like Americans." For example, MariaTe, Yolanda, and I had the following conversation after a childbirth class:

> *MariaTe:* My problem is with Andrea [a patient].
> *Natalia:* What problems do you have with Andrea?
> *MariaTe:* She is a snob and a racist. She and I went to a talk in the community and the only thing she would do is to talk bad about the women who were there. She said, "Look, they act like they just arrived from a small town." She is a racist and a classist. And I say, don't forget where you came from. Her family came here as immigrants, without papers, and she was born here. I know her parents worked hard and went back to Colombia with money . . . but anyhow.
> *Yolanda:* Yes, today in [prenatal] class she was aggressive and impatient. She has everything one needs to be arrogant in this country. She is a Latina, but she acts like an American. We have no doubt: she lets everyone know she was born here, that her boyfriend is a gringo, that she knows the language, and that she knows the culture.

> *MariaTe:* Mi problema es con Andrea.
> *Natalia:* ¿Qué problemas tienes con Andrea?
> *MariaTe:* Ella es snob y racista. Ella y yo fuimos a una charla en la comunidad y lo único que Andrea hacía era hablar mal de las mujeres que estaban ahí. Decía, "Mira, acabadas de bajar del pueblo." Es racista y clasista. Y yo digo, no niegues la cruz de tu parroquia. La familia de ella vino aquí como inmigrantes, sin papeles, y ella nació aquí. No niego que los papás trabajaron mucho y volvieron a Colombia con plata . . . pero todavía.

Yolanda: Sí, ahora en clase era agresiva, impaciente. Ella tiene todo lo que se necesita para ser prepotente en este país. Ella es latina, pero actúa como americana. De eso no nos deja la menor duda: Le deja a todos saber que es nacida aquí, que su novio es gringo, que sabe el idioma, y que conoce la cultura. (Fieldnotes)

The Latina maternity care coordinators' criticism is similar to African Americans' and Mexican Americans' accusation against members of their own racial group of "acting white" (that is, a middle-class version of white) and abandoning their community (Bettie 2003). Yolanda's reaction shows how the existence of "ungrateful" Latinas was a threat to her moral identity. The community's Latinas were supposed to be the neediest. If not, there was no need to protect them.

The view of the ideal Latina client reinforced the maternity care coordinators' view of "American" clients as "trouble." "Americans" and Latinas were often defined in contrast to one another. The maternity care coordinators claimed that "American" women complained, wasted their time, and "failed to show up." If they did show up, they often had an "attitude." "Americans" would, as one of the maternity care coordinators put it, "step on their toes" and, most important, did not show appreciation of the maternity care coordinators. These expressions of anger by the "American" clients could potentially challenge the maternity care coordinators' moral identity as health providers. However, they had the opposite effect. They made the maternity care coordinators feel more aware that their perseverance in the face of such difficulties indicated their actions were even more noble. They could thus reason that a high-paying job in a clinic with privileged clientele does not offer the same opportunities to feel good about one's work. As much as the maternity care coordinators did not enjoy "difficult" clients, they would have had more difficulty fashioning a moral identity without them.

Finally, the maternity care coordinators believed that Latina clients needed more help. They saw Care Inc. as the only viable option for Latinas. According to Melanie: "They [Americans] can get health care. A lot of our American clients qualify for Medicaid and they qualify for Medicare and there's tons of other places in the community that they can receive health care. I mean, not tons, but there's other places, you know? And we're really the only place around here that serves the Latino community. And, we have so many clients we don't know what to do with" (Fieldnotes).

Similarly, the Latina maternity care coordinators claimed that their "American" clients did not need a lot of counseling. Yolanda explained: "Yes, by the time they [Americans] see us, they already have their minds made up" (Fieldnotes). The maternity care coordinators also maintained that their "American" clients had access to all the information they needed, and this assumption shaped the way they counseled these women. I recorded how MariaTe gave the results of a pregnancy test to a 19-year-old African American woman:

> *MariaTe* (talking slowly and softly): Why did you come in today?
> *Ruth:* I came to check if I am pregnant.
> *MariaTe:* Are you taking contraceptives? Are you taking care of things?
> *Ruth:* No. I do not take any birth control methods. I have a kidney problem, so I can't take any hormones, and we are going to decide with my doctor what contraception I might use.
> *MariaTe:* Are you planning to get pregnant?
> *Ruth:* No. Not really. But if I am, well, I guess, it will be welcomed.
> *MariaTe* (in a celebratory tone, congratulating her): The results indicate you are pregnant.
> *Ruth:* Oh, OK. (Ruth's eyes begin to water. She does not seem pleased with the news.)
> *MariaTe:* Are you taking vitamins or folic acid?
> *Ruth* (shaking as tears began to fall down her face): What is that?
> *MariaTe:* Folic acid is a vitamin. It is good, and it prevents the baby from having problems when developing his spinal cord.
> *Ruth:* No. I am not taking that.
> *MariaTe:* Here, I will give you a sample bottle. Here at the clinic we offer prenatal care, do you want to get it here?
> *Ruth:* Prenatal care? (Ruth looks confused and overwhelmed.)
> *MariaTe* (talking slowly): Yes. You will be assigned a maternity-care coordinator, like me, and you will get medical care, WIC, and other state services.
> *Ruth:* I guess. (She moves her hands to her face and begins to sob.)
> *MariaTe* (concerned): Are you OK?

Ruth: Yes. (Ruth takes a Kleenex and wipes her tears off her face.)
MariaTe: Good, let's schedule the first prenatal.

When MariaTe returned, I asked, "Do you think she is OK with the news? She seemed a little shaken up by the results." MariaTe responded (her tone was concerned), "I know. Do you think I should have talked to her about abortion? But she said it would be welcomed. Well, she is American, she has all that information." MariaTe did not discuss all the options with Ruth: staying pregnant, putting the newborn up for adoption, or obtaining an abortion. Ruth appeared confused and overwhelmed with the news of being pregnant, but MariaTe ignored it. MariaTe seemed to focus only on Ruth's *literal* responses: "I guess it will be welcomed"; and "OK." Because MariaTe did not inform her of all her options, including abortion, MariaTe could not ask Ruth, should Ruth decide to terminate the pregnancy, whether she would have trouble getting access to the cash she needed to pay for the abortion. MariaTe assumed that all "Americans"—regardless of their race, age, or class—have access to information about abortion. Confronted with evidence that she provided sub-par service, MariaTe said that her actions were commensurate with the client's level of need (and maintained her positive sense of self at the same time).

This moral identity required the maternity care coordinators to provide excellent service to needier clients. Consider how MariaTe informed a Latina of her right to have an abortion; I recorded the following conversation between MariaTe and Cheli, a Latina who waited in MariaTe's office for the pregnancy test results:

MariaTe: Remember you have more options. You can always abort.
Cheli (looking at MariaTe, talking fast): Oh no! If I am pregnant I will have it. As you know, I lost one, and that is very hard. I do not know if I can handle an abortion.
MariaTe (talking slowly, putting her hand on Cheli's): It is your decision. I just wanted to give you options. But of course you can handle an abortion. It is your right to have an abortion. It can be the best option for you, since you are taking care of a newborn and also working.

(After several minutes the lab technician called MariaTe to get the results of the pregnancy test. When MariaTe returned, she said to Cheli:)

MariaTe (talking softly, with her hand on Cheli's shoulder): We are going to schedule a prenatal visit. You are pregnant.
Cheli (crying): Poor baby.
MariaTe (with her hand on her shoulder, she spoke firmly): I repeat, you have other options. You can always abort.

The maternity care coordinators did not see many African American or white clients; the majority of the women they counseled were Latinas. It would be unscientific to generalize from Ruth's case, since I observed few interactions between maternity care coordinators and African American women. However, because maternity care coordinators considered "Americans" as privileged, at least relative to Latinas, maternity care coordinators may have been less likely to give particular information to non-Latina patients.

The maternity care coordinators frequently told me that they were the only ones who cared for and about Hispanics. For example, Yolanda shared her discontent with the services provided to Hispanics at another local community clinic. To Yolanda, Care Inc. was the only realistic option for Latina clients: "You know, Hispanic clients complain a lot about [Clinic B]. They say that they are treated like dirt. . . . They are not good at giving information to the Latina women. I had one who called here asking for some information complaining that no one helped her. If they did not know the information, they should. And if they have the information, why don't they give it to them? And it is not because they are too busy. Their case load is lower than the one we have here" (Fieldnotes).

The white maternity care coordinators felt the same way. As Rachel said to me:

I think Latinas are discriminated against all the time, in particular in the area of reproductive health. I know that many people say that it was much worse in their country, where abortion is illegal. So yes, it is different here in the US, but not by much. Here [in the United States] Latinas still get denied access to

medical services. Latinas have limited options on their reproductive choices. And Latinas have to face racism and discrimination daily when going to the hospitals, going to pharmacies,
anywhere. So even if abortion is legal, for many Latinas, abortion is denied every day. (Fieldnotes)

When I asked Rachel about unfair treatment she thought her
clients faced, she spoke only of Latinas. She said in an interview:

I think there are more barriers for Hispanic women that do
not speak English, or are not a resident of the state of North
Carolina. If you do not speak English, in spite of the fact that
it is a federal law that if you have a large percentage of people
that speak a certain language that the County Social Service
Agencies are supposed to have somebody that can serve as a
translator or is preferably bilingual. Many of the counties are
in violation of that federal law. When I call the hospital, even
though a hospital swears up and down that they have many,
many translators, oftentimes a woman will go there and there's
not somebody available to help translate.

All the Care Inc. maternity care coordinators felt that Latinas and Latinos had no other health-care options and were constantly victims of
bigotry and discrimination. The maternity care coordinators described
Latinas as a "community that needs us." By helping the "neediest," the
maternity care coordinators could feel good about themselves—even
if it meant granting some clients special treatment and not others.

In sum, maternity care coordinators' construction and maintenance of moral identity was shaped by their identity categories (e.g.,
race, class, gender, nationality). The maternity care coordinators
constructed a moral identity by defining themselves as "sisterly"
and "feminist" health-care providers caring for "sweet" and "needy"
Latinas, who had to deal with "difficult" and "privileged" African
American women.

6

"Working in the Trenches"

How "Doing Good" Helps Higher-Status Staffers Build Their Moral Identity

AT CARE INC., THE TWELVE HIGHER-STATUS STAFF—all but one of whom were white—collectively interpreted their difficult work conditions as evidence that they were "heroic" workers (Joffe 1978). The difficult conditions of their work only made their moral identity—being health-care providers who helped the neediest of the needy—even more important. Their commitment to serving the underserved of North Carolina became a symbol of their dedication to fight against racism and classism.

The higher-status staffers saw themselves as promoters of equality and empowerment. They saw their work as helping and empowering those who needed them the most. They were aware of how class inequalities and racism undermine poor whites' and African Americans' health and longevity. As staff physician Dr. Carter (pseudonym) told me in an interview, "I knew I wanted to do poverty medicine, indigent medicine." Dr. Koncord, the lead doctor, emphasized how poverty undermined patients' health and care:

> Patients can't afford tests or many doctor visits. And they won't buy the medicine or they won't go to get the x-ray anyway so why order it. . . . You know, if someone is having certain kinds of bowel complaints, for instance, in an older person, a

107

colonoscopy would be what we would recommend to do. But a colonoscopy is a thousand dollars! So, if I tell someone "I think you should have a colonoscopy," unless I really make a very big deal, they won't do it. I have to make a big deal, [not] "You could do it," or "I think it would be a good idea if you do it." If I don't really say, "I think it's very important to do this. It's expensive but . . ." (Interview)

The higher-status staff defined all staff members' work—health care for the poor—as crucial. These higher-status employees implied that everyone at Care Inc. sacrificed equally for the higher good. They often talked about the importance of providing health care for "underserved populations." Dr. Koncord, a white female who had been working at Care Inc. for 22 years, told me in an interview: "I always wanted to work in a community that doesn't have enough doctors; there aren't enough doctors per capita. But I particularly wanted to work with people from the lower socioeconomic [class]. I didn't want to be in private practice and have the goal be just making a lot of money. I wanted to be able to be more focused on public service."

Another white female clinician, Dr. Toril, echoed the importance of working at a community clinic:

I always knew I wanted to do primary care and I also knew I wanted to do it with underserved people. . . . [They are] people who have a hard time getting the medical care that they need either because of language barriers, cultural barriers, but most usually economic barriers. Why do any of us do anything altruistic? Ultimately it's because we want to feel needed. . . . My clients might not get to see a doctor if they don't see me. I want to see people who might really not get medical care otherwise. They face significant barriers. (Interview)

The higher-status staffers, then, framed their work as a challenge they purposefully *sought out* because they saw it as a chance to "do good." For Gloria, the white female physician associate, the clinic enabled her to work on both primary health care for women and rural health. She explained in an interview how she viewed her job: "I feel half of the doing good is just being in the room. It's when somebody is coming to you and talking to you, treating somebody with respect, listening, touching, being compassionate, empathetic. A lot of healing can just happen right there. And then the medicine helps."

Although the higher-status staffers in the clinic were sought out to resolve disputes, they were relatively sheltered from the conflicts between lower-status African American and Latina staff. This was due, in part, to their physical segregation in other parts of the clinic, as well as the high regard the lower-status staff (African American and Latina) granted them for sacrificing more lucrative jobs elsewhere and staying to help serve the poor. By passing up higher pay to help the poor African American and Latina/o clientele of the clinic, the higher-status health-care practitioners earned a "moral" wage that consisted of esteem and sympathy (from the staff and community) and a positive self-conception in lieu of a higher salary. Higher-status workers in the clinic were seen by the staff (and themselves) as moderators and not participants in the racial tension of the clinic (regarded as a problem between the lower-status African Americans and Latinas). They were buffered both by their race *and* their occupational position as higher-status workers.

When racialized tensions ran high at the clinic, the local managers and administrators of Care Inc. organized a mandatory conflict-resolution session facilitated by two outsiders (an African American woman and a Latina). The "diversity training session" was promoted by the white human resource coordinator and the lead doctor as an occasion to "air grievances" and remind each other that clinic conflicts were a consequence of working "in the trenches" and helping the people most in need.

The higher-status health-care workers pleaded for "respect" among all workers. Their appeals for solidarity assumed that the conflicts resulted from structural constraints (such as financial problems) and the prejudices of, in their words, "a few bad apples." The higher-status workers argued that all staffers faced social, political, and economic constraints. As we will see later, they argued that, while making life more difficult, these constraints made their work even more meaningful and important. These (real) structural constraints, therefore, offered potential resources with which all staff (African American, Latina, and white workers) could fashion identities as good health practitioners. But, as shown above, this type of solidarity talk was ineffective, because the staffers did not uniformly experience the same social, political, and economic constraints. While job challenges helped Latinas and African Americans establish solidarity within their own race, their hostilities toward each other inhibited efforts to craft a moral identity based on shared interests, solidarity, and unity.

Contrary to the lower- and middle-status workers, higher-status staff framed the problems faced by health-care workers at Care Inc. in three ways: explaining problems in the clinic as inevitable and a consequence of structural constraints (e.g., "demographic changes," "resource insufficiencies," and "stress" in the workplace), which presumably affected everyone in the same way; assuming that conflicts resulted from the prejudices of "a few bad apples"; and assuming that the problems would work themselves out—thus, no policy changes were necessary and no one (in particular themselves) was to be held responsible for the tensions in the workplace.

However, as I point out, these symbolic efforts failed to address the fundamental causes of staff tension: changing racial demographics in the community, the emergence of Spanish as a primary language in the clinic, and the limited opportunities for other jobs for lower-status staff outside the clinic because of prevailing racial and class oppression. Instead of resenting these challenges, the higher-status staffers felt good about having *chosen*, as one of them put it, "to work in the trenches." In addition, for the higher-status staff in the clinic, the growing demand for medical care reflected the importance of the work they did. Inadvertently, by claiming that all workers were doing good—even heroic—work in the face of significant obstacles, they emphasized how all health-care workers were in the same boat, therefore denying how race and class inequalities were reproduced inside the clinic.

"Working in the Trenches": Structural Constraints and Normalizing Tensions

The higher-status staff in the clinic, all but one of them white, also assumed that the tensions experienced by the lower-status African American and middle- and lower-status Latina workers resulted from unavoidable structural constraints (e.g., "resource insufficiencies," "demographic changes," and "stress" in the workplace). Presumably, these constraints shaped the day-to-day care given by *all* staff—white, African American, and Latina—serving the poor of North Carolina.

Resource Insufficiencies

The staff at Care Inc. worked under difficult conditions and would have been paid more in a private organization. They were overworked, facing a continuous stream of clients. The white staffers frequently talked about how Care Inc. provided health services to people in need and how the demand for health services at the clinic exceeded the center's capacity. Many times the white staffers recalled how new clients had to wait three to six months to be seen.

In 35 years of the clinic's history, the staff doubled in size to respond to the growing and changing needs of the community. Despite this growth, Care Inc. was chronically short-staffed. All the health-care workers had too much work and complained to each other (and to me) about it. In all the units I observed, staffers performed several tasks at once, faced a constant flow of clients, and managed to meet more expectations than they could reasonably be expected to fulfill at one place and time. As one of the two receptionists told me, "the pace is relentless."

The clinic's higher-status staffers frequently mentioned how busy they were and how they did not have time to provide all the services their clients needed. At a staff meeting, Teresa, the white WIC director, said that staffers were "stressed out" by personnel shortages and that the situation "is made worse when staff is out or positions are vacant." She described what was said in the meeting in a memo sent to the administrators and unit directors (noting that this could be shared with anyone): "It was clear from the staff meeting that [the clinic's] staff are feeling stressed by the staff shortages (medical assistant, registrar, and pending center manager). . . . This is clearly noted in the breakdown of the registration system. Since that position has been vacant, other staff have not been able . . . to get the job done."

In these ways, higher-status staff emphasized that the workload and job demands were overwhelming. Being "stressed out" was expected and unsurprising. The impossible demands of their workplace were used to explain tension and staff frustrations. Rather than feel overwhelmed, the higher-status staffers prided themselves for *choosing*, as

one of them put it, "to work in the trenches." The working conditions, while materially difficult, offered symbolic opportunities to
build their moral identity (Kleinman 1996); that is, their identity as
good people was based on their role as health-care providers for the
underserved. The price they paid in terms of lower salary and limited
clinic resources (compared to private practice) was reimbursed with
a "moral" wage (akin to Dubois's "psychic" wage).

For the higher-status staff in the clinic, the growing demand for
medical care reflected the importance of the work they did. For example, Dr. Toril, a white clinician, said to me in an interview: "Part of the
problem is that our clinic doesn't ever stop accepting new clients. If we
were a private practice we'd say, "We've got as many clients as we can
handle now. We're not going to enroll any new clients, I'm sorry, and
you have to find another doctor." But there's not that other option
for our clients, and so we keep taking new clients. . . . So that's part
of the problem, it's just the way that there's too much need and not
enough resources, and that we're kind of swamped."

Refusing clients was not an option. Instead of seeing the increase
of patients as a burden, this clinician considered it a sign that her
work at Care Inc. was even more important.

The rise in client visits was, conversely, accompanied by shrinking
federal support. In the early 1970s, Care Inc. was 100 percent federally
funded; this occurred as a result of the War on Poverty in the mid-
1960s, when funding community clinics was a priority. As Care Inc.'s
African American executive director, Mr. Mackenzie, explained at the
diversity retreat, by 2004, federal grants comprised only 24 percent of
Care Inc.'s budget. The cutbacks forced the clinic, as well as others like
it, to cut costs and to "move to self-sufficiency." He explained what
this meant for the clinic: "We need to collect from clients. If we don't,
we would have to close the clinic's doors. No money, no clinic!" The
problems facing Care Inc. were not only serious, but they were also
getting worse. At the same time, the moral identity of the higher-status
staffers in the clinic was bolstered. The level of structural constraints
allowed them to feel good about themselves for doing important work.

The aforementioned white female clinician, Dr. Toril, emphasized
in an interview that she provided medical care to "people who face
significant barriers" and that the clinic's staff cared for underserved
people despite "the need outstrip[ping] our resources." For her,

these working conditions were a source of pride. But for the lower-status staff, such working conditions did not have the same effect. They signaled more job insecurity and fewer health-care options for members of their own communities. Federal funding cuts may have helped the higher-status staffers see their sacrifices as more noble, but they reminded the African American and Latina workers how fragile their positions in the clinic were.

Demographic Changes

The higher-status staff in the clinic interpreted the increasing percentage of Latina/o clients as an opportunity to help an entirely new population. Becky, the human resources coordinator, said to me in an email: "The [clinic] has gone through a rapid change from being a primarily African American clinic to today largely Hispanic, as evidenced by the most recent client numbers indicating that Hispanics make up 67 percent of the clients. As a community health center, we respond to the clients who appear in our waiting room."

Similarly, Rachel, the white director of the maternity care coordinators, stressed the importance of their Hispanic clients' need in relation to their "American" counterparts: "The question is: Where is the direst need or the highest-need area? There are many resources in this community for pregnant American women, so it's not such a priority for us to have a childbirth class in the clinic in English. . . . I really wish we could offer it, but the reality is that if we did, we would not have time to do other things and provide other very needed services. So, it is a matter of what is a priority" (Fieldnotes). Thus, by helping what one maternity care coordinator called "the neediest of the needy," Rachel derived even more satisfaction from her work.

In addition to appeals to rally around the clinic as it faced such a dire situation, the higher-status staff invoked "the changing demographics" as an opportunity for solidarity among clinic workers. The fact that many of their Latina/o clients were undocumented provided them with an opportunity to help "needier" clients. They asserted that this made their work even more important. Dr. Koncord, the white female lead clinician, said in an interview: "[W]hen I first started working, I would say there were virtually no Hispanic clients. . . . Occasionally some would come in without translators, but it was just very, very rare. . . . In general people who came to the clinic were native-born US. . . . I would guess that at least 50 percent of the clients I see now are Hispanic, maybe more. On walk-in days, it's almost 100 percent. . . . I am happy that we're serving the Hispanic community. I think it's their right. It's good that we're doing that."

The community had a clear need for services targeting the growing Latina/o population. Care Inc.'s staff worked hard to fill that need with limited resources. This enabled positive feelings for the higher-status staffers providing the work. They saw it as a common ground from which group solidarity could emerge. The lower-status African American staffers, however, interpreted these same demographic changes, and the accompanying language barriers, as a threat to their jobs and their community, making it harder for them to feel that they were "in the same boat" as the white and Latina staff.

The demographic change did not adversely affect the white higher-status workers, as they all spoke Spanish. In addition, the higher-status workers also felt more righteous and self-sacrificing, given the greater cultural and economic gap between them and the population they served. For them, this made the shifting demography of the clients a positive change; and of course, these higher-status health-care providers were shielded structurally from the work flow and the majority of the difficult working conditions.

Stress

The white staffers were aware that it was difficult for some staff (and clients) to adjust to the changing demographics and resource insufficiencies at the clinic. For example, the lower-status African American female staffers watched as the clientele shifted from 80 percent African American to more than 60 percent Latina/o in a matter of years. The higher-status staff acknowledged that the lower-status African American and Latina workers were experiencing stress and frustration. African American staff complained that the clinic was overlooking the needs of the surrounding African American community because of the needs of newly arrived Latinas/os.

Dr. Toril, one of the white female clinicians, linked the staff's daily struggles to provide health care to the tensions at the clinic: "I worry that we are talking about stress in the workplace, meaning that we work in a place where the need outstrips our resources. We're always being asked to do more, and more, and more, and more. And not just the doctors; the nurses, the receptionists, the pharmacist—everybody. And that stress and the tension that that brings, and the way that it makes people snap at each other. . . . It's just a perfect setup for resentment" (Interview).

At Care Inc., stress was the natural response to increasing structural constraints; "everybody" felt it. Stress in the workplace, this clinician explained, went with the demands of each worker's role. For example, she described the receptionists as "up there all by themselves without support, being asked to do a really, really hard job." Becky, the white human resources coordinator, echoed in an interview how overworked everyone was: "Because we're so lean, everybody is very stressed out. Everybody is wearing three and four hats." Besides too much work, the needs of the clients were also seen as overwhelming.

Dr. Carter, another white female clinician, also mentioned in an interview how stressful providing health care for the underserved was: "I think just because we do indigent medicine we deal with high-stress stuff." She later elaborated: "[A] stressful day would be a day where a lot of patients came in with psychosocial issues, which take a lot of time and you never feel like you do enough for them or give them the resources that they need. And those are hard days when you have three or four people who really needed attention, that you could have spent a lot of time with going through their social issues and just didn't have the time, so you had to cut visits short and reschedule and maybe not have gotten some of the time with them that you wanted."

The psychosocial issues, she explained, included, "Things like domestic violence, things like depression, their anxiety disorders or just issues where women are, especially Latino women, tend to have a very different lifestyle here; you know—where in Mexico their life was very social, and they were up and moving around and always visiting other people. They can get very, very isolated in the United States and really not leave the house most days."

For Dr. Carter, the isolation Latina/o clients felt made them "needier" and increased the level of stress clinicians felt when providing health care for the underserved.

In an interview, Dr. Toril also mentioned how stressful it was to provide health care to the poor:

> [I]t's pretty stressful to have fifteen minutes to see someone and address so many issues. And I often felt a little bit over my head, because family doctors shouldn't be seeing elderly people, because there are a lot more problems that an internist would see. . . . And our patients have always been very reluctant to see specialists, because they either don't have insurance or they don't want to go to the hospital or Medicare doesn't cover it. They might have Medicare, but they don't have supplementary insurance. So, they really don't want to go to a specialist. . . . So, I was handling more complex problems than I might have in a different setting. So, there was certainly a lot of stress with that.

It is true that the speeding-up of the workload and not turning away clients affected all the workers at Care Inc. It was harder for the lower-status African American and Latina staffers, however, because they had fewer resources to deal with the strains. As lower-status workers, they were paid the least, were overworked, and dealt with high turnover among fellow staffers. The lead clinician acknowledged this: "I wish that the clinic had the resources to pay people better and that salaries were—well, to pay people better and to hire more. The non-professional staff is really stressed out and understaffed and underpaid." In this context, the lower-status workers, in particular, felt besieged by the sped-up working conditions and the increased volume of people they served on a daily basis; they were expected to perform several tasks at once while facing a continuous stream of clients. Unlike the higher-status staff, the lower-status staff was not physically segregated behind doors and curtains from the incoming clients, who had to wait while being admitted and processed. Whereas clients were relieved to finally see the doctor or clinician, the waiting room was a less peaceful and satisfying place. Clients often took out their frustrations on the lower-status African American and Latina staff in their immediate presence.

Additionally, it was harder for lower-status workers to feel good about workplace stress when budget cuts at Care Inc. resulted in worsening social services that their communities relied on. Unlike the higher-status white staff, Care Inc. clients were also members of the same communities as the lower-status staff. Few white clients of any class level—only 17 percent of the clinic's client base—came to Care Inc. The higher-status staffers were sheltered from race and class inequality inside and outside the clinic. The lower-status staffers, however, were on the front lines, forced to accept firsthand the challenge of decreased funding for social services.

Mr. Mackenzie, the African American executive director who did not work inside the clinic, did acknowledge that racial tension existed. As an executive director, it was his job to help solve workplace conflict. He did this, in part, by invoking the inevitability of stress and change during his speech at the diversity workshop: "We are going through a lot of changes, all out of necessity. I know the changes are pissing some of you off. We are not done with the changes. We try hard to be a family and to be there for people who need us. . . . It ain't easy to merge people and culture. It is hard work" (Fieldnotes).

For him, the frustration and conflicts at Care Inc. resulted from the sacrifice all workers made for the higher good: caring for the underserved in North Carolina. He drew on these conflicts to attempt to create and reinforce a sense of purpose among the workers at Care Inc. and to promote a sense of unity. However, the extent to which people can sacrifice depends on the options and personal resources available to them (Kleinman 1996). While the higher-status white staffers at Care Inc. may have seen their job as a "calling," the lower-status African Americans and Latinas saw it as part of a larger struggle that did not end when they returned home at the end of the day.

In sum, the higher-status workers' allusions to these challenges suggested that difficult working conditions affected everyone in the same way (and were a consequence of "working in the trenches" and helping the people most in need). For example, Gloria, the white female physician associate, told me in an interview that "working in the trenches" was what made her happy: "I worked in international health research for ten years. And then I came back to [Care Inc.] after being in international research. I wanted to get back into the trenches. . . . It's the real world . . . you are in the hole; not only looking at the hole. I prefer being in the hole. . . . I really enjoyed traveling and working in HIV prevention in Latin America and the Caribbean. It was wonderful work. But that was another time, and now it's this time, and I'm happy to be doing this."

For her and other higher-status white staffers, working with the less-privileged members of the community who might otherwise "fall through the cracks" lent importance and gravitas to the work. She believed that she and those like her were on the front lines, seeing and softening the daily impact of insurance-industry policies and immigration reforms on human lives.

The white clinicians assumed that "not everyone can do this work" because it "takes a special kind of person" to endure the difficulties of being community health-care providers. One white female clinician, Dr. Toril, explained in an interview: "I work there because I feel called to work there. . . . God called me to medicine to the underserved. It's really what I've always wanted to do. . . . I think that the camaraderie that I have with most of my colleagues—especially the other providers, but many of the nurses, too—it's kind of like being in the trenches together, kind of like the battlefield. This is an impossible, overwhelming job, but aren't we good people for getting it done?. . . We're doing something worthwhile together."

She and the other higher-status staffers used the real structural constraints to confirm their self-image as "special," caring people. The series of conflicts—resource insufficiencies, demographic changes, an overwhelming pace, and too many things to do in a day's work—provided evidence of how stressful working at the clinic was, and how everyone had it "so hard." By interpreting the clinic as a "battlefield," merely surviving was seen as a sign of success worthy of self-satisfaction. The joy of survival, however, is amplified for those who altruistically volunteered for the sort of job that would make them feel "special."

"A Few Bad Apples"

The higher-status staffers also appealed for "tolerance," especially at the conflict-resolution session. Their pleas for solidarity among workers assumed that the conflicts were incited by the racial prejudices of, as they said to me in interviews, "a few bad apples." The higher-status staffers claimed that the conflict could be resolved if only workers would simply try to get along. They believed that if all the lower-status workers could understand that the interpersonal conflicts stemmed from the difficult personalities and the racial prejudices of a few, things would improve (regardless of the ongoing problems posed by race and ethnicity).

One of the biggest points of contention among the African American and Latina staff was the increased use of Spanish in the clinic. Some African American staffers had complained to Dr. Koncord, the white female lead clinician, that they felt disrespected, criticized, and made fun of because they did not know (or were unwilling to learn) Spanish. Dr. Koncord listened to these complaints and suggested during a staff meeting that English be spoken in such settings as the lunchroom. The Latinas interpreted this policy change as a betrayal and as further evidence that the African American staff had disproportionate influence within the clinic. The higher-status white staffers in the clinic interpreted this tension as evidence of clashing personalities and feelings of insecurity as a result of not being included in conversations.

For example, Dr. Koncord defined the tensions at Care Inc. in colorblind terms, as a product of the exclusion that some co-workers felt. She explained:

> The non-Hispanic staff of the clinic feels that when people are talking, they don't know what they are talking about. They don't know Spanish and they wonder if they are talking about them [the non-Latina staffers]. They feel left out. Nobody feels comfortable in the lunchroom, because they are speaking Spanish, and others, in other tables, are speaking English. Non-Spanish-speaking people feel disrespected when Spanish is being spoken. They feel that they don't count, and that they are excluded intentionally. . . . Some non-Spanish [-speaking] people [are] feeling like they have been here for a long time, and they [used to] fit in, and now they don't fit in anymore. And I have even heard that some English speakers feel that some co-workers criticize them for not knowing Spanish: "You have been working here for five years and why don't you speak Spanish?" So, I think that mostly everyone wants to feel included, and we tend to make each other feel excluded. (Fieldnotes)

At Care Inc. all the higher-status white staff spoke Spanish. For the most part the African American staff did not speak Spanish. So while Dr. Koncord referred to "non-Hispanic staff," she really meant only the lower-status African American staff. However, she recognized that it worked both ways: each group (African Americans and Latinas/os) felt excluded. Eventually, the white lead clinician acted as mediator and manager of what she interpreted as the fragile emotions of upset workers. She said that she felt that the "Spanish-speaking staff" misunderstood her intentions. She said that "they were never told they could not talk with each other in Spanish, although that is what they heard." She said: "Hispanics feel they want to talk Spanish with each other. . . . Hispanics also feel like they have been ridiculed by co-workers about their accent, and that people come up to them and say 'Stop talking that crap,' and 'Talk in English.' I also heard that clients sometimes treat them rudely because they don't talk good English, and I guess there is a sense that they do not have any power in the clinic" (Fieldnotes).

In an attempt to address these issues, Dr. Koncord wrote a letter to the staff that read, in part: "I was so struck in speaking with many of you, how deep the hurt and polarization runs. I was equally impressed by how similar everyone's needs and wishes are. . . . I was struck by the unintended hurt caused by cultural misunderstandings. What gives me hope is that much of what we all want is the same: to feel included, to feel comfortable together, and to share respect and power in our work community."

Again, she focused on how both groups—non-Spanish-speaking and Spanish-speaking workers—had similar "feelings of exclusion." Both groups felt hurt and polarized.

It is not unusual for whites to define racial conflicts in emotional, individualistic, and apolitical terms (Bonilla-Silva 1997, 2001, 2003; Carr 1997). According to Bonilla-Silva (2003), whites tend to insist that race does not matter in the post–civil rights era, and explain racial inequality and racial segregation as the outcome of non-racial matters such as market dynamics, naturally occurring social phenomena, and the cultural deficiency of certain minority groups (2). Racial minorities, accordingly, are responsible for social inequality and are charged by many whites with "playing the race card" (1).

At Care Inc., the white health-care providers discussed racial conflicts in such terms. When I asked Catherine, a young white social worker, about "the language issue" and the tensions among workers at the clinic, she said: "It is not racism. No one here, in my opinion, is a bad person. No one is racist. I think it is a problem of irreconcilable differences. It is all about personalities." Similarly, Liz, the white center manager said: "In my opinion, the problem is the personality of some specific people. They are just difficult, and not easy to get along with, yet work together." And Becky, the white human resources coordinator, explained: "I think that the complaints people have about some staff people—that, by the way, are very few—are things they do to anyone and everyone. It is what I would call equal-opportunity rudeness." Becky implied that those few people were also rude to higher-status workers at the clinic. The lead clinician, Dr. Koncord, agreed: "I believe that what is going on is, in part, the normal interpersonal conflict that arises in an organization. . . . But these persons they are complaining about are rude to everyone, regardless of their race, or language [she laughs]. But many people are assuming that it is because of the racial differences. This is sad, but it is not about the differences . . . because they forget that they are not kind to anyone" (Fieldnotes).

All these higher-status staffers described "the problem" as caused by the abrasive personalities of a small number of people. Becky, the human resources coordinator, characterized the problem as caused by a "few bad apples." They described these people as difficult, hard to get along with, and unkind to everyone. Individualizing the problem also served to quarantine it and assign blame to a few individuals. When probed, these higher-status workers identified the rude people as: "You know, the receptionist [that] people always complain about," "The triage nurse we had to let go," "The woman in medical records, who sometimes is difficult with co-workers," and "I have heard that some people have problems with the two medical assistants who do not speak Spanish, you know." They never mentioned the names of these five women, all of whom were African American. The white staff only referred to them by their roles. It is conceivable that the white staff avoided mentioning the workers' race so as not to appear racist. The white staff also asserted that these women—the five "difficult" lower-status African American staff—were rude to everyone, and not just lower-status staffers and Latina/o clients. Yet, I never observed these five women talking back or being rude to white staff. In my experience, these "problematic" women were only "difficult" with Latina co-workers and Latina/o clients.

The tension between African Americans and Latinas in the clinic affected the white staffers, but they did not feel they were directly involved. Instead, they saw their role as peacekeepers. It took them some time to realize that class-based and race-based conflict even existed in the clinic. For example, Dr. Carter, a white female clinician, said: "When I found out there was a problem, I was absolutely shocked. . . . I think that is going to be an ongoing issue when you have primarily Spanish-speaking staff that are mixing with people who do not want to learn Spanish, but who want to be able to understand what's going on around them and might feel a little paranoid about somebody speaking, you know, people speaking Spanish close by" (Interview).

Although she does not mention them by name, it was clear that this clinician was speaking about the African American staff. She also blamed these women for the tensions at the clinic because they "do not want to learn Spanish." But the higher-status staff in the clinic did not directly intervene. No one was ever warned, disciplined, or sanctioned for being "rude" to a co-worker.

The absence of tangible penalties can be explained, in part, by the same moral identity that allowed the higher-status staffers to feel good about themselves and their work. This identity was dependent upon their ability to be caring, understanding, and forgiving. Sanctioning the "problematic" staff, who were all African American, might expose higher-status staffers to charges of racism and unfairness, and of taking sides with one group at the other's expense.

There was only one instance in which a "problematic" staffer was fired. This occurred in an extreme situation and involved direct harm to a white patient. The staff member was the African American triage nurse. She denied a girl access to a clinician just before the child began convulsing and had to be taken to a local hospital emergency room. Latina staff had previously lodged complaints about her with the center manager, the lead clinician, and the human resources coordinator. Latina/o clients lodged complaints as well, but it took several months and frequent complaints before she was reprimanded. Only after the director of an allied Latino/a organization documented the complaints he received about Care Inc. from Latina/o clients was she asked to meet with the lead clinician and strongly encouraged to change. Ultimately, she was fired. The racial tensions at Care Inc. were escalating, and the administration felt it had to step in and take action.

"It Isn't Really Our Problem!"

The higher-status staffers also assumed that the problems would work themselves out, and thus no policy changes were necessary and no one, in particular themselves, was to be held responsible for the tensions in the workplace. This was made evident by what happened after the mandatory "diversity workshop" organized by the higher-status staffers.

Shortly after the triage nurse was fired, the higher-status staffers organized a "diversity workshop" facilitated by two outsiders (an African American woman and a Latina). The higher-status staff, administrators, and the African American executive director were principally the ones who spoke. As it turned out, the session was a symbolic attempt to address the problems at the clinic, but it did not result in any real policy changes or in assigning responsibility to anyone. Although the facilitators had numerous recommendations for the clinic once the workshop was over, they told me afterward in interviews that these recommendations were never put into effect.

The African American facilitator shared with me a memo she prepared with some solutions she would have proposed to the administrators of the clinic (had they asked):

> Need for cross-cultural and anti-oppression training among staff. There should be consistent consequences for treating co-workers and clients disrespectfully or rudely. These consequences should be evenly applied regardless of race/ethnicity, organizational status, or position. The organization needs to diversify its staff at all levels, but it should create rules that support all staff regardless of race or ethnicity, getting needed help from existing staff until diversity exists. The line of authority for staff in the hierarchy should be respected. However, there

needs to be sensitivity to and respect for clients' need to relate
to someone who may better understand their particular needs;
staff needs to have a clear explanation of each other's role, and
their job training and performance expectations.

The two facilitators, African American and Latina alike, were
disappointed that their insights were not taken more seriously by
the higher-status administrators at Care Inc. The African American
facilitator reflected:

> They threw away this little bit of money and said to themselves:
> "It's done now." . . . When I went back to follow up, for exam-
> ple, and gave them some of the implications of what people said
> and some of the things that I thought that they seriously could
> do that had no financial implications. . . . [i]t was almost like
> a courtesy meeting. . . . Until they can get the commitment at
> the top to do certain things differently it's moot, 'cause certain
> things that are problematic really need the power and the influ-
> ence of those folks at the top to really do something. (Interview)

The Latina facilitator echoed this assessment in an interview: "The
exit interview got postponed. Didn't seem to be a top priority to get
that information. They didn't want to hear what the problems were
and what it took to start doing something to change the clinic. My
perception was that [Care Inc.'s] attitude is a little bit 'Well, we're
going to leave it in the hands of the local folks to follow up.' That's
sort of the message I got: 'Don't expect us to call you except if we can
make arrangements for this one meeting. So, thank you very much.'"

In interviews, the facilitators said that the white staffers saw themselves not as a part of the "problem" at the clinic, but as "problem-
solvers." The Latina facilitator said: "They [white staff] acted like it
wasn't really their problem. One of the doctors was listening to the
radio or something like that. A couple of times I felt like saying, 'You
know, you are a big part of the problem!' Only the doctor that is in
charge of the clinic, she seemed to really feel acutely that it was, in
part, her responsibility to find the solution. And she looked pained
a lot of the time to me. So, I feel like they were at a loss as to why
there were problems."

The African American facilitator had similar views of the white staff at the clinic:

> In terms of the whites that I met in the center, I really got a sense that they didn't see themselves as part of the problem. . . . [The center manager] said that it is the Latinos' and the African Americans' problems that might need to be fixed, not that we have decisions that we can make at the top level that will help resolve some of this and that we [whites] have some role in it. I saw them more as outside. They were analyzing it from outside and seeing that there were things that needed to be fixed between the folks. . . . They sat on the fence. (Interview)

The facilitators' comments confirm observations of the higher-status staffers at the clinic as desiring that the "diversity workshop" would create an opportunity for lower-status staff to "air grievances." Simply talking about the problem and making appeals for solidarity based on a shared moral identity, however, was not the same as committing to change or taking some responsibility for the problem.

In sum, the higher-status health-care providers collectively interpreted their difficult work conditions as proof that they were "heroic" workers. Their commitment to serving the underserved and poor of North Carolina became a symbol of their dedication to be "moral" doctors, and the growing demand for medical care reflected the importance of the work they did. The higher-status health-care workers saw their work as helping and empowering those who needed them the most. Rather than resenting these hurdles, the higher-status staffers felt good about having *chosen* "to work in the trenches."

Inadvertently, the higher-status staffers' construction of "the moral self," overlooked the economic and social powerlessness (Allan, Mayo, and Michel 1993; Flynn and Fitzgibbon 1996) experienced by African American and Latinas within and outside the clinic. They unintentionally considered less important the daily struggles of their minority co-workers. Finally, the higher-status health-care providers, by emphasizing how all health-care workers were in the same boat, denied how race and class inequalities were reproduced inside the clinic.

7

Moral Identity Construction and New Ethnic Relations

THIS BOOK EXPANDS UPON OUR UNDERSTANDING of moral identity and how it intersects with race, class, and gender, especially in the workplace. I have illustrated how the health practitioners of Care Inc. construct and maintain a moral identity in concert with how they categorize themselves and others along racial and class lines, in addition to gender and nationality.

The staffers crafted their moral identity by drawing on the cultural resources (Einwohner, Hollander, and Olson 2000; Williams 1995) available to them. For instance, the lower-status African American staffers constructed a moral identity by defining themselves in opposition to what they perceived Latinas/os to be. The African American staff labeled Latina staff as "lazy" and incompetent workers who lowered the clinic's status and respectability. They criticized Latina clients for being bad mothers, blamed Latina/o clients for "working the system," and considered them irresponsible care-seekers who were undeserving of subsidized health care in the United States. As a result, African Americans perceived their work as important: they had to prompt Latinas to be better workers and to protect Care Inc. from potential abuse by Latina/o clients.

The lower-status Latina health-care providers also viewed their work as important, but for different reasons. Latina staff told me that they needed to protect Latina/o clients from suffering indignities at the hands of the African American staff and needed to make sure

126

African American staffers did not take advantage of them nor deny them health care.

The mid-level staffers—the maternity care coordinators—constructed a moral identity by defining themselves as "sisterly" and "feminist" health-care providers caring for "sweet" and "needy" Latinas, who had to deal with "difficult" and "privileged" African American women.

The higher-status staff, all of them white except one, constructed a positive self-image by defining health-care work as heroic, explaining problems in the clinic as inevitable and a consequence of structural constraints that presumably affected everyone in the same way, and assuming that conflicts resulted from the prejudices of "a few bad apples."

This analysis suggests that moral-identity construction is an active process. The health-care practitioners' moral-identity construction is shaped by demographic changes in the clinic's clientele as the result of immigration, as well as the social, economic, political, and cultural contexts in which they are working and subsequently fashioning their identities. They collectively interpret their difficult work conditions, which vary by race and class of the health-care practitioner, as evidence that they are "heroic" workers (Joffe 1978). The difficult conditions of their work, as well as the status of their positions, only add to their challenges and give their moral identity (being health-care providers who helped the underserved of North Carolina) added importance. However, the workers' construction of the "moral self" and "moral client" identities had unintended consequences.

Constructing Moral Identity: Shaping Ethnic Relations and Social Membership

Sabotage

One potential consequence of the way staffers constructed their moral identity is sabotage. At the clinic, as mentioned before, administrators asked African American staff to train Latina staff. If the African American staff sabotaged that training, the Latina's job might have been in jeopardy. The racist and sexist images of Latinas as "lazy" would become a self-fulfilling prophecy.

This happened to Barbara. After working for six months at Care Inc., she had not been trained to do all the procedures required of a medical assistant. She was supposed to be trained by Desiree, the African American lead nurse, and Eva, an African American medical assistant. Barbara explained:

Well, I guess you can say Desiree has trained me, but there is a lot that is missing. She still has to show me how to check a child's vision, how to take blood to check sugar or hemoglobin levels—many things are missing. But at least they let me do something, and time goes by. But I still do not do everything.

And I am on probation! Eva and Genesis do not collaborate with me, and if I have any doubts or questions they ignore me. They only criticize, get mad when I ask them to do something when I can't, and they constantly tell me I am slow. Also, I feel ashamed, especially with the doctors. Because many times, most of the time, they ask me to do something and I have to tell them that Desiree has not trained me. I do not want them to think it is my fault or I am lazy. It is not my fault. I want to learn, but if they do not tell me how to do it, how can I do it?

Se puede decir que Desiree me entrenó, pero falta mucho. Falta que me muestre cómo chequear la vista de los niños, como se saca sangre para chequear el azúcar y la hemoglobina, falta muchas cosas. Al menos me dejan hacer algo, y se pasa el tiempo. Pero todavía no hago todo.

¡Y estoy en prueba! Eva y Genesis no me colaboran y si tengo dudas o una pregunta ellas se hacen de la vista gorda. Solo critican, se ponen bravas cuando me toca decirles que hagan algo porque yo no puedo, y dicen todo el tiempo que soy lenta. Además, me da pena, especialmente con las doctoras. Porque muchas veces, la mayoría de las veces, si me piden que haga algo, y no sé hacerlo, o no me han entrenado para hacerlo, me toca decirles que Desiree no me ha entrenado. No quiero que piensen que es culpa mía o que soy perezosa. No es mi culpa. Yo quiero aprender, pero si no me dicen cómo hacerlo, ¿como puedo hacerlo? (Interview)

The lack of training was taking a toll on Barbara. She was worried she would get fired. This was not the only way Barbara's effectiveness at work was being limited by African American staff. Because Eva "trained" Barbara, she was also asked to monitor and evaluate her performance. If Eva's assessment of Barbara's work was negative, this could have serious consequences: termination or no more overtime. This is what happened to Barbara. As she recalled in an interview:

> I was doing overtime, on Saturdays. They called me to say that they were not going to give me more overtime because I do not qualify. They said to me that a co-worker, from here, not a supervisor, had called to say that I had not completed my training. Then I said to them, "Look, that is not my fault. I want to learn. And moreover," I said to them, "if you want, as we are here late on Wednesdays and I have to stay here, you can finish my training. Nobody has trained me, and that was Eva and Desiree's responsibility. And Eva goes and tells them that I am not qualified!" And I cannot tell anything to Desiree, the supervisor, because they are such good friends. She does nothing!

> Yo estaba haciendo el overtime, el sábado. Me llamaron para decirme que no me iba a dar el overtime porque yo no calificaba. Me dijeron que una trabajadora de aquí, no la supervisora, les dijo que todavía no había completado el training. Entonces le dije, "Mira, eso no es mi culpa. Yo tengo todo el interés de aprender. Y es más," le dije, "si tú quieres, como aquí los miércoles estamos tarde y tengo que quedarme aquí podemos terminar mi training. Nadie me hace el training, y eso le correspondía a Eva y a Desiree. ¡Y va Eva a decirles que no estoy calificada!" Y no puedo decirle nada a Desiree, la supervisora, porque son tan amigas. ¡Ella no hace nada!

Other staff at the clinic also commented that Eva "had it in for Barbara." For example, Angela, an African American laboratory technician, said to me in an interview: "I know that Eva does not like Barbara. I have heard how she talks about her, tells her she's too slow, tells her in a rude way she was doing something wrong, or . . . even if Barbara was doing it right, she would have something to say about it. Eva is always watching what time she comes in, what time she leaves. Being very judgmental. If you don't like somebody you'll come up with something, you'll make them look bad or, 'She's not doing that right . . . she's too slow.'"

The way lower-level staffers constructed their moral identity put Latinas' jobs in jeopardy, as some African American staff sabotaged their training. Another of the strategies health-care providers used to maintain their moral identity was to put racial and ethnic boundaries into effect.

Enforcing Racial Boundaries

Another strategy health-care practitioners used to fashion their moral identity was constantly differentiating, in negative ways, between African Americans and Latinas/os. Racist stereotypes for African Americans and Latinas/os rely upon racial solidarity and fixed racial boundaries (Winant 2004). The lower-status health-care practitioners—African American and Latinas—constructed friendships and alliances based on their shared racial-ethnic identity with their co-workers. The moral-identity construction processes used by the women of color in Care Inc. strengthened the racial alliances (Scott 1998).

But when a person appeared to be of mixed race, this alliance was called into question. For racism to exist, one race needs to see the people of the same race as looking alike. People who can "pass" as one race or another call the concept of race (and their supposed corresponding personality traits and/or assumed alliance) into question. "Passing" refers to a person, classified as a member of one racial or ethnic group, choosing to identify with another racial or ethnic group. Usually, passing refers to a mixed-race person who, by "looking" and "acting white," is absorbed into white society. This process is possible in the United States because any non-European ancestry marks a person as different, and thus a mixed-race person is not "really white," but is just "passing" for white (Bonilla-Silva and Embrick 2005).

At Care Inc. some of the African American staffers assumed that members of their race needed to look alike (and if they did not look alike, they needed to act alike). Any staffer who did not look "black" or did not fulfill community obligations was categorized as "not-black," and as "acting Latina." As Bonilla-Silva (2001, 41) explains: "Because races are socially constructed, both the meaning and the position assigned to races in the social structure are always contested. Who is to be black or white or Indian reflects and affects the social, political, ideological and economic struggles among the races."

The distinctions made between staffers who looked and acted black and those who did not helped African American staffers maintain their group image as "good workers" (and Latinas as "lazy") and distance themselves from the Latinas (i.e., they do not "look" or "act" like us). These presumed racial/ethnic traits become the crucial grounds for connection and solidarity, and for resistance by African Americans to the experience of "Latinas/os taking over" Care Inc. (Scott 1998).

Consider the example of the one staff member whose racial identity was in question by her co-workers at Care Inc. Angela was a light-skinned African American lab technician, who many clients assumed was Latina. Desiree (the African American lead nurse), Eva (an African American medical assistant), and Genesis (an African American medical assistant) did not get along with Angela. Because of Angela's light skin, Eva often asked her: "What are you? Why do you look the way you do? Are you really black? I cannot tell you from Bibiana. You look Hispanic!" Angela said that some African American staff thought she was trying to pass for Latina. In an interview, Angela said: "I was holding a Hispanic baby, the mother was having a procedure done, and Eva comes up and starts picking at the baby, you know, kind of playing with it or something. And Desiree walks up and the baby starts crying, and she said, 'Oh, the baby wasn't crying with you, it must think you're Hispanic too—doesn't like black people.' I'm thinking, it's a little bitty baby, the baby doesn't know."

The dislike that Desiree, Eva, and Genesis had for Angela became evident in the way they treated her when she needed medical attention. Angela was in her early 30s and had had a partial hysterectomy when she was 22. Four years later she had a complete hysterectomy. In June 2003, Angela started bleeding, and had surgery in September 2003 because she had "a third ovary and it had popped through the vagina and attached to the intestines and bladder" (Fieldnotes). Angela bled heavily, urinated on herself, and was in a lot of pain before her surgery. Angela reported that Desiree, Eva, and Genesis did not believe that she was sick or in pain, even when she told them, repeatedly, how she felt. Angela said to me:

> Desiree and Eva were not helpful. They thought I was playing, or not as sick as I was. They thought I was making it all up. They never knew how much I was suffering. They even made fun of the way I was walking. But I was in such pain. I could not stand up straight, and many days I could not even walk. Eva would shout, "Straighten up, straighten up!" . . . And I technically only took four weeks off. Desiree called me at home every day after the surgery and asked me: "When are you coming back, when are you coming back?" When I did not answer the phone because I did not want to be bothered, she would leave a message that went like this: "You must be out, which means you must be better. So come back." (Fieldnotes)

Angela confided in Bibiana and Barbara (both Latina staff) and me about how sick she felt and the hostility she experienced from her African American co-workers. The reactions of Desiree, Eva, and Genesis make sense within a context where racial groups are expected to stick together and act alike (Scott 1998; Tatum 2003). Deviating from racial norms calls the authenticity of those norms into question (Chafe 2001). The African American women on staff garnered much of their status from seniority and their strength in numbers. Their seniority was difficult to challenge; but if Angela did not identify with the African American staff, their collective influence suffered.

Angela was aware of how the African American staff was struggling to maintain racial boundaries within the clinic. She feared she was seen as betraying her race by siding with the Latina staff. She said to me during a break:

> Eva doesn't want to learn Spanish and doesn't want to help me when I am doing labs for a Hispanic client. I can ask Bibiana and Barbara for a word and they will write it down, or something. But I have to ask Bibiana and Barbara to write it down when Eva is not around. She gets very upset when we all get together for lunch or they help me out. I am trying my best to learn Spanish.

But if you don't speak good English, then Eva is, "She doesn't speak good English, she needs to speak better English." That bothers me, 'cause that's your language, I feel, well, speak it. 'Cause we're speaking our language, might as well speak yours. That bothers me. I don't expect Bibiana to speak without an accent, and I understand her fine, but some people say, "Oh, I don't understand her." Well, take your time and listen to her. People are impatient; that's what I think. (Fieldnotes)

Perhaps because she was marginalized by the African American staff in the clinic, Angela was the only African American staff member who viewed her own racial group as contributing to the racial tensions at Care Inc. She said:

I think because there's more Hispanic workers who are speaking to the Hispanic community that's coming in, and the Americans that are there, have been there, I guess, from the beginning, and they're really set on not changing. The white people that are there are the doctors, and only one [white] doctor doesn't speak fluent Spanish. I think she should only see American-speaking clients, because she's pulling the nursing staff away to translate for her. And then you have the black staff. Desiree, she speaks basic stuff, like me I guess, basic. Which is OK, because she gets the point across and she can understand. Eva speaks not a word, Margaret doesn't speak a word, and that's kind of . . . I guess they're afraid they'll lose their job, but . . . they don't like change. That's the only thing I can think of, it's a big change issue, and a job-security issue. If you're going to hire Hispanic people you . . . have to realize if they don't speak English . . . that . . . you're going to have to give them time, because you're not even speaking Spanish. I don't speak Spanish properly, very well—broken Spanish, probably even wrong. At least I'm trying; they're not even putting forth the effort. (Fieldnotes)

Angela understood why African Americans resented Latinas/os. She recognized that African American staff members were unhappy about the increase in the Latina/o population in North Carolina, and the changes it forced upon the clinic and the demands it created on the workers. Angela also recognized that African American staff feared losing their jobs.

African American staff feared that Latinas/os would surpass them in the racial hierarchy, improving their social standing and accessing privileges in the United States by being adopted into white society. As Gold (2004, 956–957) explains:

> A considerable body of recent scholarship on whiteness argues that a wide range of national and ethnic populations now accepted as white were initially racialized when they first entered the United States as immigrants (Doane and Bonilla-Silva 2003). However, it was European origin groups who were able to improve their social standing and access to privileges in US society by adopting the social, economic, and ideological practices of the white majority while simultaneously separating themselves from and denigrating blacks (Gerstle 2001; Jacobson 1998; Roediger 1991). Some evidence suggests that Asians and light-skinned Latinos are currently making progress in that direction (Lee, Bean, and Sloan 2003). However, few if any African origin people have achieved whiteness in American society.

The African American staff's negative reaction to Angela demonstrated this: She was light-skinned and often taken for a Latina. For some African American staff, Angela may have represented a threat from Latinas/os, even though she was a light-skinned African American woman. Just as Angela could "pass" as Latina, this might imply that light-skinned Latinas could pass as white (which could potentially be even more threatening to the lower-status African American women on staff).

Limiting Access to Patients of the Other Race

Finally, the last potential consequence of the way staffers constructed their moral identity was in limiting patients of the other race to access to health care. Most of the African American staff maintained that African Americans clients' interests and needs were no longer a priority at Care Inc. Stephanie, the African American triage nurse, often mentioned that "other blacks" in the community asserted that the "clinic is catering to Latinas/os," and "they [Latinas/os] are why all the black clients have left or were driven away."

For Margaret, the African American receptionist, the problem was that the clinic had disproportionately hired Latina health-care workers to accommodate the increase in Latina/o clients. She said in an interview: "You know, I think people should have a doctor or a nurse or a health-care provider who they feel comfortable with. For many, and for me, that is a person that speaks English, and might look like me. And many feel that now [the] staff is Hispanic. They don't like that. They complain to me at the front desk. And I've even had some clients say, 'If Dr. So-and-So wasn't such a good doctor, I would go elsewhere, but I've had her or him for years.' To me, it's a problem."

However, several African American staffers believed that Latinas/os clients "worked the system," trying to get health care when it was not needed. After she had seen a white mother and her six-year-old daughter, Stephanie (the African American triage nurse), commented to me:

> See, Natalia, this mom did not embellish. She just stated the facts. This is why I let her see the doctor. Why do they, Mexicans, want their children to be sick? Why do they want the kids to be seen by the doctor? I feel sorry for the child [presumably referring to a Latina six-year-old we had seen earlier that morning], because the mom was coaxing her to say that she was sick. I asked her to say the truth . . . and I asked her if she could eat, drink, and she said yes. She said she did not feel sick. So, I did not let them see the doctor. . . . The problem is the moms. Some get hostile if they can't get in. And it is a problem only with the Mexican community. . . . I don't understand it, but there is something wrong with their idea of what it is to be a mom. (Fieldnotes)

Prevailing rhetoric by African American staffers regarding Latinas/os and immigration describes a battlefield of contested resources where African Americans are out to protect what was previously theirs and Latinas/os are seeking to exploit any available social service. For example, Stephanie felt obligated to protect the clinic from Latina/o clients who seemed to "work the system" and under false pretenses seek medical care for their children (to the point of coaxing their children to lie and pretend they are sick to ensure that they are seen by a clinician). Latina/o clients must have the "right" social skills that will enable them to deal with her, which Stephanie defined as "being nice to me." Stephanie is thus a gatekeeper. For example, after a Latina woman and her two sons left her office, she said to me:

> I can't let them see a doctor if they are not willing to tell me what is wrong with them. They don't want to see me, just the doctor, and I can understand that. But, they have to see me since it is my job to decide if they can get in or not. So like it or not, they have to deal with me. And the way to get to see a doctor is to be nice to me. If they do not want to talk to me, then it is likely they won't get through. (Fieldnotes)

In this case, protecting a precious community service was easier for Stephanie because she interpreted her gatekeeper actions as defending the clinic from exploitive parents. Stephanie's comment that "they won't get through" is an example of her wielding power, power that she can exercise depending on her race-framed perception of the client.

Latino fathers were not exempt from "bad" parent imagery. In one instance, I was asked to translate for Antonio, a 33-year-old Latino, who wanted to complain to the center manager about his visit with Stephanie. He began:

> This is the second time I have come to this clinic. The first time I brought my daughter, and today I brought my son. When I brought my daughter, I came because the school asked me to pick her up, because she needed to be seen by a doctor. Today, like the last time, the nurse asked me why I had come, and what my son had. I am not a doctor or a nurse, so I do not know what my son has. I know he has a fever, but I do not know how high. After that, she, in a very impolite way told me to go to the hospital, that they could not see us. I always have problems with her, and I do not know why. And it's only with her that I have problems. I give thanks that she [looking at me] and others treat me like an equal, and make me feel human.

Esta es la segunda vez que vengo a esta clínica. La primera vez vine a traer a mi hija, y hoy vine a traer a mi hijo. Cuando traje a mi hija, vine porque el colegio llamó y me dijo que la recogiera, pues ella necesitaba ver a un médico. Hoy, como esa vez, me preguntó la enfermera por qué vine, que, qué era lo que tenía mi hijo. No soy médico, ni enfermera, y por lo tanto no sé que es lo que tiene mi hijo. Sé que tiene temperatura, pero no sé cuánto. Después ella, en una forma muy despectiva me dijo que fuera al hospital, que no me podían ver. Siempre tengo problemas con ella, y no sé por qué. Y siempre es con ella que tengo problemas. Doy gracias que aquí ella [mirándome a mí] y otras me trata como un igual y me hace sentir humano. (Fieldnotes)

Antonio was not the first Latino/a client to complain about the treatment she or he received at the clinic. It was common for Latinas/os to complain to the Latina staff, in particular the two Latina maternity care coordinators, the Latina receptionist, and the Latina lab technician, about the African American staff mistreating them. These complaints were then made known to the center manager and the rest of the staff, either in person or at staff meetings. Still, the disrespect of Latinas/os by some of the staff—the same African American staff members—continued.

At the same time, Latina staff at Care Inc. also called upon racialized rhetoric—of African Americans as rude and demanding—in describing black clients' behavior at the clinic. When I asked Tatiana, the Latina receptionist, "What has been your experience with black clients at the clinic?" she replied:

> **Tatiana:** Black people are demanding. White people are not. White people are educated, the majority. Black people, they expect a lot of me, of us. They do not want to give you their identification card. For example, I say to them, "May I have your card, please?" "I don't have it." They say it in a very arrogant manner. I say to them, "Well, I need some information to file in the computer. It's going to take me longer than what you think if you don't help me." Then they say to me, "What do you want me to do? I've been here a hundred times." I say to them, "Well, I don't know you by name. I've seen you before,

but I don't know you by name. What's your date of birth?" I
speak to them as they speak to me. . . . So I think that black
people are more demanding. Even more rude.

Natalia: And the white people are not like this?

Tatiana: No. White people are more gracious. More educated.
They say "thank you," they say "please." Black people don't say
"thanks" or "please." Very little.

Tatiana: Los morenos son demandantes. La gente blanca no
lo es, la gente blanca es educada, la mayoría. Los morenos, ellos
como que esperan mucho de uno, de ti. No te quieren dar la
tarjeta. Por ejemplo, le digo, "May I have your card, please?"
"I don't have it." Pero así bien déspotas. Le digo, "Well, I need
some information to file in the computer. It's going to take me
longer than what you think if you don't help me." Entonces me
dicen, "What do you want me to do? I've been here a hundred
times." Le digo, "Well, I don't know you by name. I've seen
you before, but I don't know you by name. What's your date
of birth?" Yo le hablo como ellos me hablan. . . . Entonces se
me hacen más demandantes los morenos. Aún más groseros.

Natalia: ¿Y los blancos no son así?

Tatiana: No. La gente blanca es más consciente. Más educada.
Te dicen "Thank you," te dicen "por favor." Los morenos muy
poco saben decir "gracias" y "por favor." Muy poco. (Fieldnotes)

African Americans and Latinas identified problems at Care Inc.
as a result of personality flaws associated with racial groups. These
shared understandings made it easier for African Americans and Latinas to favor their own racial group in terms of care and make sure
their fellow race/ethnic members got to see a doctor. This resulted,
ultimately, in an unequal quality of health care delivered to clients.
The actions of both African American and Latina health-care workers reinforced racism, sexism, and class inequalities (Johnson 1997).

The health-care practitioners' construction of the identities of the
"moral self" and the "moral client" had unintended consequences;
namely, it enabled the lower- and mid-level status staffers to give
preferential treatment to some clients over others and still feel good
about themselves and their work. The African American staff saw

themselves as needing to protect the African American community, which was under siege because of the influx of needy Latina/o immigrants and the shrinking of resources. The lower-status African American staff did not act out of malice, but instead exercised an unspoken triage of their own: Who were the neediest of the needy? For them, it was the African American clientele that had once predominated at the clinic.

Conversely, the lower- and mid-level Latina staff saw themselves as those called upon to "save" Latinas from African Americans who (they believed) were prejudiced against them. Under these conditions, differential levels of health-care service did not threaten their moral identity, it emboldened it. By seeing African American patients as (relatively) privileged, the lower- and mid-level Latina staffers saw themselves as doing whatever they could to protect a vulnerable population: Latinos/as.

This pattern of progressive people failing to notice how they inadvertently reinforce the inequalities in their midst has been found in other groups and organizations. Kleinman (1996), in her ethnography of an alternative health center, found that the white men "saw themselves as having transcended the divisions created by gender, credentials, and social class. . . . But . . . social and economic arrangements . . . as well as ingrained ideas about gender and credentials led members to treat each other unequally" (124). She found that the male practitioners were at the top of the workplace ladder while the staff and volunteer women were at the bottom of what was supposed to be a non-hierarchical organization. The men in this center had most of the power and influence, and were revered and cared for by the women who served as the staff and volunteers. These women were grateful to have the opportunity to care for the men, who benefited from these arrangements. Kleinman found that inequities were masked, in part, because members shared a moral identity that made them feel good about themselves. As Kleinman wrote (138): "Participants in progressive social movements may believe, like members of Renewal, that taking on the moral identity of leftist, antiracist, or feminist is enough. Participants may assume that membership in the group guarantees that they have purged themselves of the sexism (or racism, classism, heterosexism) that permeates the society 'out there.' But as the case of Renewal shows, people cannot will away years of ingrained ideas about who deserves more respect, resources, and affection. Many inequalities may thus be reproduced beneath conscious awareness."

Therefore, as Kleinman concludes (140), it is important for people to see their identities "as a symbol of a lifetime commitment to critical self-reflection and radical action. . . . Without such self-examination we may think of ourselves as progressive, but fail to build a better alternative."

This happens, too, within African American groups and organizations. Elaine Brown (1992), in her memoir *A Taste of Power: A Black Woman's Story*, describes the sexist acts of men in the Black Power movement. The African American (heterosexual) men gave more importance to challenging white racism and reduced the importance of sexism and other inequalities. African American activist women responded by forming antiracist movements in which gender inequalities were considered fundamental.

Similarly, research by Prindeville (2003) on Native American and Latina women activists and leaders found that Native women's activism tends to advance the well-being of the Native American community as a group rather than the needs of Native American women in particular, and as a result "gender equality is less important an issue for Native women than tribal sovereignty, for instance, which defines their very survival as a people and incorporates the preservation of Native culture, lands, religious beliefs, and language"(601–3). Ford (1990, 88) explained "that there is an interdependence, a complementarity, between [Native American] men and women and that until their group has equality with other ethnic groups, they, as women, will not gain." Conversely, gender identity seemed more salient for Latina/o leaders and public officials, in part because Latino society traditionally has been characterized as patriarchal, making such leaders and officials more concerned with challenging sexism and altering existing patriarchal systems to allow for greater equality and participation by women in all facets of society (Prindeville 2003, 606).

Discussion

In the foregoing study of Care Inc., I analyzed how a number of structural mechanisms made working there more challenging and less satisfying for *some* of the staff: the training and supervision of Latina staff (almost exclusively by the more senior African American staff); the "gatekeeping" positions several of the African American staffers held (e.g., the African American triage nurse and the African American receptionist deciding who could see a provider), which gave the African American staff some power over the mostly Latina/o clients; and the lobbying by some African American staffers to require all staff members to speak only English when not interacting with Spanish-speaking clients.

Given these inequalities, I then explored how the construction of "moral identity" among health-care practitioners divided lower-status workers along racial/ethnic lines, reinforced racial boundaries, and influenced who was served at Care Inc. The strategies devised to craft and maintain the staffers' moral identity were shaped by their class and racial/ethnic group membership. The higher-status staffers, all but one of them white, collectively interpreted the difficult working conditions as evidence that they themselves were "heroic" workers. The mid- and lower-status Latina staffers felt Latina/o clients were especially "needy" and deserving of special protection; guarding over them was a crucial component of their moral identity. However, the moral identity of African American staffers was threatened, as they could not base their identities on serving "their people" because the client population had become Latina/o. African American staffers crafted a "worthier" self-image by depicting Latinas as lazy, working the system, having no regard for rules and discipline, and being bad and irresponsible parents.

The health-care practitioners' construction of the identities of the "moral self" and the "moral client" had unintended consequences, because it enabled the lower- and mid-level staffers to give preferential treatment to some clients over others while still feeling good about themselves and their work.

In North Carolina, as described above, health-care staffers play an important role in shaping the membership and integration of Latina/o immigrants into society, as these newcomers' engagement in community life is determined, in part, by how they interface with health-care staffers and other public-service staffers, as well as with state officials (Deeb-Sossa and Bickham-Mendez 2008). Latina/o immigrants' visible participation in community life in "el Nuevo

South" is most regulated in the health-care center through eligibility requirements.

The focus of this work, with regard to eligibility requirements, was to understand how social membership is constructed and enforced in this institutional setting. Health-care clinic staffers interpret and apply policies in ways that define who is entitled to public services and goods. In short, then, these clinic staffers define who is a worthy patient. As Deeb-Sossa and Bickham-Mendez (2008) contend, health-care workers, and in particular the gatekeepers within community health-care clinics, often construct "otherness" through their enforcement of eligibility requirements. The institutional organization of health care gives certain groups more power in defining and enforcing membership. At Care Inc., the structural organization of the community clinic and the gatekeeper positions assigned to African American staffers facilitated the marginalization of Latina/o patients. The roles of receptionist and nurse held by these African American staffers facilitated their regulation of access to health care.

The African American receptionist and nurses exercised considerable power over patients' access to health care at Care Inc. The African American triage nurse saw all patients who came without an appointment and decided who could be seen that day. Both the African American receptionist and nurses believed that Latina/o patients "worked the system," sought unnecessary medical care for their children, and "refused to learn English." The combination of Latinas/os' poor English skills with the African American staffers' preconceived view that immigrants "abuse the system" justifies, in their view, limiting this group's access to adequate health-care services (Deeb-Sossa and Bickham-Mendez 2008). As the authors conclude, "The institutional positions of gatekeepers in social services and clinics place them in the role of enforcers of borderlands. Socio-cultural markers such as race and language skills, as well as institutional ones such as Social Security numbers and state-issued forms of identification become 'badges' of social membership, indicating entitlements and social inclusion" (625).

The determination of who was a worthy patient was shaped by these health-care workers' race and ethnicity, gender, class, and nationality. Such determination was also shaped by how it helped them create and maintain a sense of value (moral identity) about their work, despite difficult working conditions. These processes ended up, as described above, reproducing workplace inequalities by dividing lower-status workers, enforcing racial boundaries, and limiting access to health care for patients of the "other" race (Hirsch 2003; Konrad et al. 1998).

Health-care staffers (mostly women) at community clinics have the capacity to determine who is allowed to receive prompt care and who must wait—defining and maintaining borders of social membership (Anzaldúa 1987, 107; Deeb-Sossa and Bickham-Mendez 2008, 631)—by using race as an exclusionary device. The exclusion of immigrants does not primarily occur due to individually held racist beliefs; rather, it occurs because of institutional mechanisms, such as eligibility requirements, that contribute to the marginalization of immigrants and to the enforcement of borders of social inclusion.

The African American staffers at Care Inc., given their gatekeeping positions at this community clinic, were assigned the role of border enforcers. As a result, these gatekeepers used socio-cultural markers such as race and language skills as ways of determining access to health care. Gatekeeping, together with maintaining a sense of value in their work despite changing demographics, fostered at Care Inc. a constant negative differentiation between African American and Latina staffers that influenced, also in negative ways, the care given to clients of the other race. As described before, Konrad et al. (1998) found that in private practices, health-care workers' assumptions about uninsured mothers and those who were Medicaid recipients meant that these groups encountered the most difficulty in accessing medical care for their children. My analysis of Care Inc. similarly demonstrates that health-care workers' negative attitudes toward uninsured and Medicaid patients increased and strengthened the hurdles to health care that these patients already faced.

Structurally or institutionally, white and African American staffers, via their status and job responsibilities in the clinic, acted as key gatekeepers to health care and as enforcers of social membership. They used racial and cultural markers, including language differences, to identify and categorize Latinas/os as "others" (Schwalbe et al. 2000). The construction of otherness and the enactment of marginalization by African American health-care workers—despite their low status and relative lack of authority in other situations—demonstrates how members of groups who are oppressed can make use of power to impede Latinas/os' (or any "othered" group) access to health care.

To the outside observer, it thus appears ironic that the mission of Care Inc.—to serve those with the greatest need, regardless of race or other factors—was undermined, as the unintended consequences of so many social dynamics played out on the field of moral-identity construction. Good people with good intentions fell back on racial and cultural stereotypes that ultimately kept them from "doing good" by serving the clients who needed them most. This suggests that workers who use their structural or institutional position differently—drawing on, as Kleinman (1996) suggests, "critical self-reflection and radical action"—might be key allies in the struggle for Latinas/os' access to health care, for immigrants' inclusion and integration into society, and for challenging racism. Community and workplace-based educational efforts that promote understanding and respect between newcomers and longtime residents/natives might be a worthy and effective way to channel the creation of moral identities into building alliances and promoting social change.

References

Acury, T., C. Austin, S. Quandt, and R. Saavedra. 1999. "Enhancing community participation in intervention research: Farmworkers and agricultural chemicals in North Carolina." *Health Education and Behavior* 26:563–578.

Adair, Vivyan C. 2000. *From broodmares to welfare queens: A genealogy of the poor woman in American literature, photography and culture.* New York: Garland Publishing.

Agency for Healthcare Research and Quality. 2008. "Hospital emergency departments treat mostly poor children." *AHRQ News and Numbers*, Rockville, MD, May 22. http://www.ahrq.gov/news/nn/nn052208.htm (accessed November 26, 2010).

Allahyari, Rebecca Anne. 2000. *Visions of charity: Volunteer workers and moral community.* Berkeley: University of California Press.

Allan, Janet, Kelly Mayo, and Yvonne Michel. 1993. "Body size values of white and Black women." *Research in Nursing and Health* 16:323–33.

Anti-Defamation League. 2006. http://www.adl.org/learn/ext_us/david_duke/background.asp?LEARN_Cat=Extremism&LEARN_SubCat=Extremism_in_America&xpicked=2&item=david_duke (accessed June 23, 2012).

Anzaldúa, Gloria. 1987. *Borderlands/La Frontera.* San Francisco: Aunt Lute Books.

Anzaldúa, Gloria, and Cherríe Moraga. 2002. *This bridge called my back: Writings by radical women of color.* Berkeley, CA: Third Woman Press.

Bartky, Sandra Lee. 1990. *Femininity and domination: Studies in the phenomenology of oppression.* New York: Routledge.

Bayne-Smith, Marcia, Yvonne Graham, and Sally Guttmacher. 2005. *Community-based health organizations: Advocating for improved health.* New York: Wiley.

Bettie, Julie. 2003. *Women without class: Girls, race and identity.* Berkeley and Los Angeles: University of California Press.

Blumer, Herbert. 1969. *Symbolic interactionism: Perspective and method.* Berkeley: University of California Press.

Bonacich, Edna. 1972. "A theory of ethnic antagonism: The split labor market." *American Sociological Review* 37:547–559.

Bonilla-Silva, Eduardo. 1997. "Rethinking racism: Toward a structural inter-pretation." *American Sociological Review* 62:465–80.

Bonilla-Silva, Eduardo. 2001. *White supremacy and racism in the post–civil rights era.* Boulder, CO: Lynne Rienner Publishers.

Bonilla-Silva, Eduardo. 2003. *Racism without racists: Color-blind racism and the persistence of racial inequality in the United States.* Lanham, MD: Rowman & Littlefield.

Bonilla-Silva, E., and D. Embrick. 2005. "Black, honorary White, White: The future of race in the United States." In D. Brunsma, ed., *Mixed messages: Multiracial identities in the color-blind era,* 33–48. Boulder, CO: Lynne Rienner Publishers.

Broadway, Michael J., Donald D. Stull, and Bill Podraza. 1994. "What happens when the meat packers come to town?" *Small Town* 24 (4): 24–28.

Browder, Cullen. 2006. "Immigration debate focuses on DWI fatalities." WRAL .com, November 10. http://www.wral.com/news/local/story/1088494/ (accessed November 26, 2010).

Brown, Elaine. 1992. *A taste of power: A Black woman's story.* New York: Pantheon Books.

Butter, Irene, Eugenia Carpenter, Bonnie Kay, and Ruth Simmons. 1985. *Sex and status: Hierarchies in the health workforce.* Washington, DC: American Public Health Association.

Camarota, Steven. 2004. *The high cost of cheap labor: Illegal immigration and the federal budget.* Washington, DC: Center for Immigration Studies, 2004.

Caplan, Paula J. 1998. "Mother-blaming." In *"Bad" mothers: The politics of blame in twentieth-century America,* edited by Molly Ladd-Taylor and Lauri Umansky, 127–43. New York: New York University Press.

Carbado, Devon W. 1999. *Black men on race, gender, and sexuality: A critical reader.* New York: New York University Press.

Carr, Leslie G. 1997. *"Color-blind" racism.* Thousand Oaks, CA: Sage Publications.

Chafe, William. (1977) 2001. "Sex and race: The analogy of social control." In *Race, class, and gender in the United States: An integrated study,* edited by Paula S. Rothenberg, 535–549. New York: Worth Publishers.

Charmaz, Kathy. 2000. "Grounded theory: Objectivist and constructivist methods." In *Handbook of qualitative research,* 2nd ed., edited by Norman Denzin and Yvonna S. Lincoln, 509–535. Thousand Oaks, CA: Sage Publications.

Chavez, Leo R. 2001. *Covering immigration: Popular images and the politics of the nation.* Berkeley: University of California Press.

Chong, Nilda. 2002. *The Latino patient: A cultural guide for health care providers.* Yarmouth, ME: Intercultural Press.

Clawson, Rosalee A., and Rakuya Trice. 2000. "Poverty as we know it: Media portrayals of the poor." *Public Opinion Quarterly* 64:53–64.

Collins, Karen Scott, Dora L. Hughes, Michelle M. Doty, Brett L. Ives, Jennifer N. Edwards, and Katie Tenney. 2002. *Diverse communities, common concerns: Assessing health care quality for minority Americans.* New York: The Commonwealth Fund. http://www.commonwealthfund.org/publications/ publications_show.htm?doc_id=221257 (accessed November 26, 2010).

Collins, Patricia Hill. 1999. "The meaning of motherhood in Black culture." In *The Black family*, edited by Robert Staples, 157–166. Belmont, CA: Wadsworth Publishing Co.

———. (1990) 2000. *Black feminist thought: Knowledge, consciousness, and the politics of empowerment.* New York: Routledge.

———. 2004. *Black sexual politics: African Americans, gender, and the new racism.* New York: Routledge.

Conley, Dalton. 1999. *Being Black, living in the red: Race, wealth, and social policy in America.* Berkeley: University of California Press.

Couto, R. A. 1991. *Ain't gonna let nobody turn me round: The pursuit of racial justice in the rural South.* Philadelphia: Temple University Press.

Cravey, Altha J. 1997. "The changing South: Latino labor and poultry production in rural North Carolina." *Southeastern Geographer* 37 (November): 295–300.

Dalaker, Joseph. 2001. U.S. Census Bureau, Current Population Reports, Series P60-214, *Poverty in the United States: 2000.* Washington, DC: U.S. Government Printing Office.

Darity, William A., and Samuel L. Myers Jr. 1998. *Persistent disparity: Race and economic inequality in the United States since 1945.* Cheltenham, UK: Edward Elgar.

Deeb-Sossa, Natalia. 2007. "Helping the 'neediest of the needy': An intersectional analysis of moral-identity construction at a community health clinic." *Gender & Society* 21 (5): 749–772.

Deeb-Sossa, Natalia, and Jennifer Bickham-Mendez. 2008. "Enforcing borders in the nuevo South: Gender and migration in Williamsburg, VA and the Research Triangle, NC." *Gender & Society* 22 (5): 613–638.

Doane, Ashley W., and Eduardo Bonilla-Silva, eds. 2003. *White Out: The continuing significance of racism.* London: Routledge.

Douglas, Susan J., and Meredith W. Michaels. 2004. *The mommy myth: The idealization of motherhood and how it has undermined women.* New York: Free Press.

Du Bois, W. E. B. 1903. *Souls of Black folk: Essays and sketches.* Chicago: A. C. McClurg & Co.

———. (1935) 1998. *Black reconstruction in America: An essay toward a history of the part which Black folk played in the attempt to reconstruct democracy in America, 1860–1880.* New York: Free Press.

Easterbrook, Michael, and Jean P. Fisher. 2006. "Health care costly for immigrants." *Raleigh News & Observer*, March 1. http://www.newsobserver .com/1155/story/412836.html (accessed April 2, 2006).

Economic Report of the President. 2005. Washington, DC: United States Government Printing Office.

Einwohner, Rachel L., Jocelyn A. Hollander, and Toska Olson. 2000. "Engendering social movements: Cultural images and movement dynamics." *Gender & Society* 14 (5): 679–699.

Feagin, Joe R. 1991. "The continuing significance of race: Anti-Black discrimination in public places." *American Sociological Review* 56:101–116.

Feagin, Joe R., and Karyn D. McKinney. 2002. *The many costs of racism.* Lanham, MD: Rowman & Littlefield.

Fields, Jessica, Martha Copp, and Sherryl Kleinman. 2006. "Symbolic interactionism, inequality, and emotions." In *Handbook of the sociology of emotions*, edited by Jan E. Stets and Jonathan H. Turner, 155–178. New York: Springer Science + Business Media, LLC.

Fink, Leon. 2003. *The Maya of Morganton: Work and community in the nuevo New South.* Chapel Hill: University of North Carolina Press.

Fiscella, K., P. Franks, M. P. Doescher, and B. G. Saver. 2002. "Disparities in health care by race, ethnicity, and language among the insured: Findings from a national sample." *Medical Care* 40 (1): 52–59.

Fiscella, K., P. Franks, M. R. Gold, and C. M. Clancy. 2000. "Inequality in quality: Addressing socioeconomic, racial, and ethnic disparities in health care." *JAMA* 283 (19): 2579–2584.

Flynn, Kristin, and Marian Fitzgibbon. 1996. "Body image ideals of low-income African American mothers and their preadolescent daughters." *Journal of Youth and Adolescence* 26:615–31.

Ford, R. L. 1990. "Native American women activists: Past and present." Unpublished PhD manuscript, Southwest Texas State University.

Frye, Marilyn. 1983. *The politics of reality: Essays in feminist theory.* Freedom, CA: The Crossing Press.

Gay, Claudine. 2006. "Seeing difference: The effect of economic disparity on Black attitudes toward Latinos." *American Journal of Political Science* 50 (4): 982–997.

Gerstle, Gary. 2001. *American crucible: Race and nation in the twentieth century.* Princeton, NJ: Princeton University Press.

Giddens, Anthony. (1981) 2001. "The class structure of the advanced societies." In *Social Stratification*, 2nd ed., edited by David B. Grusky, 152–162. Boulder, CO: Westview Press.

Gilens, Martin. 1996. "Race and poverty in America: Public misperceptions and the American news media." *Public Opinion Quarterly* 60:515–41.

———. 1999. *Why Americans hate welfare: Race, media and the politics of antipoverty policy.* Chicago: University of Chicago Press.

Goffman, Erving. 1959. *The presentation of self in everyday life.* New York: Doubleday.

———. 1961. *Asylums: Essays on the social situation of mental patients and other inmates.* New York: Anchor Books.

———. 1974. *Frame analysis: An essay on the organization of experience.* New York: Harper & Row.

Gold, Steven J. 2004. "From Jim Crow to racial hegemony: Evolving explanations of racial hierarchy." *Ethnic and Racial Studies* 27 (6): 951–968.

Grusky, David B., and Jesper B. Sorensen. 1998. "Can class analysis be salvaged?" *American Journal of Sociology* 103:1187–1234. Reprinted as "Are there big social classes?" in Grusky (2001) *Social stratification: Class, race, and gender in sociological perspective*, 2nd ed., 183–94. Boulder, CO: Westview Press.

Hall, Elaine J. 1993. "Smiling, deferring and flirting: Doing gender by giving 'good service.'" *Work and Occupations* 20 (4): 453–466.

Hays, Sharon. 1998. *The cultural contradictions of motherhood.* New Haven, CT: Yale University Press.

Heath, Melanie. 2003. "Soft-boiled masculinity: Renegotiating gender and racial ideologies in the Promise Keepers movement." *Gender & Society* 17 (3): 423–444.

Hemming, Jill, A. J. Rouverol, and A. Hornsby. 2001. *Neighborhood voices: New immigrants in northeast central Durham.* Durham, NC: Laser Image Corporate Publishing.

Hirsch, Jennifer S. 2003. *A courtship after marriage: Sexuality and love in Mexican transnational families.* Berkeley: University of California Press.

"History and introduction to [Care Inc.] perinatal program." Internal document of the community clinic; author collection.

Hochschild, Arlie R. 1983. *The managed heart: Commercialization of human feeling.* Berkeley: University of California Press.

———. (1989) 2003. *The second shift.* New York: Penguin Books.

Holden, Daphne. 1997. "'On equal ground': Sustaining virtue among volunteers in a homeless shelter." *Journal of Contemporary Ethnography* 26:117–45.

Holstein, James A., and Gale Miller, eds. 1993. *Reconsidering social constructionism: Debates in social problems theory.* New York: Aldine de Gruyter.

Horowitz, Ruth. 1997. "Barriers and bridges to class mobility and formation." *Sociological Methods and Research* 25 (4): 495–538.

Howard, Judith A. 2000. "Social psychology of identities." *Annual Review of Sociology* 26:367–393.

Hughes, Everett C. 1958. *Men and their work.* Glencoe, IL: Free Press.

———. 1971. *The sociological eye.* Chicago: Aldine Atherton.

Hutchinson, Earl Ofari. 2006a. "Immigration makes strange bedfellows." *AlterNet*, May 3. http://www.alternet.org/story/35801/immigration_makes_strange_bedfellows/?page=entire (accessed November 26, 2010).

———. 2006b. "Why so many Blacks fear illegal immigrants." http://www.huffingtonpost.com/earl-ofari-hutchinson/why-so-many-blacks-fear-i_b_14472.html (accessed November 26, 2010).

———. 2007. "Why Blacks march against illegal immigration—and why they shouldn't." *New America Media*, June 21, 2007. http://news.newamericamedia.org/news/view_article.html?article_id=bedb04d502d6a7af148fd569fa2247fb (accessed November 26, 2010).

Hyde, Katie, and Jeffrey Leiter. 2000. "Overcoming ethnic intolerance." *The Journal of Common Sense* 5 (Winter): 14–19.

Jacobson, Matthew Frye. 1998. *Whiteness of a different color: European immigrants and the alchemy of race.* Cambridge, MA: Harvard University Press.

Jewell, K. Sue. 1993. *From mammy to Miss America and beyond: Cultural images and the shaping of U.S. social policy.* New York: Routledge.

Joffe, Carole. 1978. "What abortion counselors want from their clients." *Social Problems* 26 (1): 112–121.

———. 1986. *The regulation of sexuality: Experiences of family planning workers.* Philadelphia: Temple University Press.

Johnson, Allan G. 1997. *The gender knot: Unraveling our patriarchal legacy.* Philadelphia: Temple University Press.

Johnson, James H., Jr., Karen D. Johnson-Webb, and Walter C. Farrell Jr. 1999. "Newly emerging Hispanic communities in the United States: A spatial analysis of settlement patterns, in-migration fields and social receptivity." In *Immigration and opportunity: Race, ethnicity and employment in the United States,* edited by Frank D. Bean and Stephanie Bell-Rose, 263–310. New York: Russell Sage Foundation.

Kaiser Family Foundation/Pew Hispanic Center. 2003. "2002 national survey of Latinos." www.kff.org/kaiserpolls/loader.cfm?url=/commonspot/security/getfile.cfm&PageID=14274 (accessed November 26, 2010).

Karjanen, David. 2008. "Gender, race, and nationality in the making of Mexican migrant labor in the United States." *Latin American Perspectives* 35 (1): 51–63.

Kasarda, John D., and James H. Johnson Jr. 2006. *The economic impact of the Hispanic population on the state of North Carolina.* Kenan-Flagler Business School, University of North Carolina at Chapel Hill. http://www.kenan-flagler.unc.edu/assets/documents/2006_KenanInstitute_HispanicStudy.pdf (accessed November 26, 2010).

Kasarda, John D., and James H. Johnson Jr. 2007. *The economic impact of the African American population on the state of North Carolina.* Kenan-Flagler Business School, University of North Carolina at Chapel Hill. http://www.kenan-flagler.unc.edu/assets/documents/2007_KI_AfricanAmerican_Study.pdf (accessed November 26, 2010).

Kaufmann, Karen M. 2003. "Cracks in the rainbow: Group commonality as a basis for Latino and African-American political coalitions." *Political Research Quarterly,* 56 (2): 199–210.

Kiefer, Christie W. 2000. *Health work with the poor: A practical guide.* New Brunswick, NJ: Rutgers University Press.

Kleinman, Sherryl. 1996. *Opposing ambitions: Gender and identity in an alternative organization.* Chicago: University of Chicago Press.

———. 2007. *Feminist fieldwork analysis.* Thousand Oaks, CA: Sage Publications.

Kleinman, Sherryl, and Martha A. Copp. 1993. *Emotions and fieldwork.* Newbury Park, CA: Sage Publications.

Konrad, T. R., S. J. Clark, G. L. Freed, R. Schechtman, and J. Serling. 1998. "Does insurance coverage affect infants' access to immunization services from community medical practices? A simulated patient telephone study in three states." Abstract book, Association for Health Services Research, annual meeting, 1998. http://gateway.nlm.nih.gov/MeetingAbstracts/ma?f=102234067.html

Lambert, Wallace E., and Donald M. Taylor. 1990. *Coping with cultural and racial diversity in urban America*. New York: Praeger Publishers.

Lee, Jennifer, Frank Bean, and Kathy Sloane. 2003. "Beyond black and white: remaking race in America." *Contexts* 2 (3): 26–33.

Leidner, Robin. 1999. "Emotional labor in service work." *Annals of the American Academy of Political and Social Science* 561 (1): 81–95.

Levenstein, Lisa. 2000. "From innocent children to unwanted migrants and unwed moms: Two chapters in the public discourse on welfare in the United States, 1960–1961." *Journal of Women's History* 11 (4): 10–33.

Lofland, John, and Lyn H. Lofland. 1995. *Analyzing social settings: A guide to qualitative observation analysis*, 3rd ed. Belmont, CA: Wadsworth.

Mani, Lata. 1990. "Multiple mediations: Feminist scholarship in the age of multinational reception." *Feminist Review* 35:24–41.

Massey, Douglas S. 2008. *New faces in new places: The changing geography of American immigration*. New York: Russell Sage Foundation.

McCall, George J., and J. L. Simmons. 1978. *Identities and interactions: An examination of human associations in everyday life*. New York: Free Press.

McClain, Paula D., Niambi M. Carter, Victoria M. DeFrancesco Soto, Monique L. Lyle, Jeffrey D. Grynaviski, Shayla C. Nunnally, Thomas J. Scotto, J. Alan Kendrick, Gerald F. Lackey, and Kendra Davenport Cotton. 2006. "Racial distancing in a southern city: Latino immigrants' views of Black Americans." *The Journal of Politics* 68:571–584.

McIntosh, Peggy. 1997. "White privilege and male privilege: A personal account of coming to see correspondences through work in women's studies." In *Race, class, and gender: An anthology*, edited by Margaret L. Andersen and Patricia Hill Collins, 76–87. Belmont, CA: Wadsworth.

McMahon, Martha. 1995. *Engendering motherhood: Identity and self-transformation in women's lives*. New York: Guilford Press.

Mead, George Herbert. 1934. *Mind, self, and society*. Chicago: University of Chicago Press.

Mies, Maria. 1986. *Patriarchy and accumulation on a world scale: Women in the international division of labour*. London: Zed Books.

Mills, Charles W. 1997. *The racial contract*. Ithaca, NY: Cornell University Press.

Mindiola, Tatcho, Yolanda Flores Niemann, and Néstor Rodríguez. 2002. *Black-brown relations and stereotypes*. Austin: University of Texas Press.

NACHC (National Association of Community Health Centers). 1996. *America's health centers: Quick facts*. Washington, DC: NACHC.

North Carolina Census Data. 2007. *http://quickfacts*.census.gov/qfd/states/37000.html (accessed November 26, 2010).

North Carolina Institute of Medicine. "Expanding health insurance coverage to more North Carolinians: North Carolina Task Force on Covering the Uninsured: April 2006." http://www.nciom.org/projects/uninsured/uninsured.html (accessed September 12, 2006).

Omi, Michael, and Howard Winant. 1994. *Racial formation in the United States: From the 1960s to the 1990s*, 2nd ed. New York: Routledge.

Passel, Jeffrey S., and Roberto Suro. 2005. "Rise, peak, and decline: Trends in US Immigration 1992–2004." Washington, DC: Pew Hispanic Center. http://pewhispanic.org/files/reports/53.pdf (accessed November 26, 2010).

Peacock, James L., Harry L. Watson, and Carrie R. Matthews. 2005. *The American South in a global world.* Chapel Hill: University of North Carolina Press.

Pedriana, Nicholas, and Robin Stryker. 1997. "Political culture wars 1960s style: Equal employment opportunity-affirmative action law and the Philadelphia plan." *American Journal of Sociology* 103 (3): 633–691.

Pew Hispanic Center. 2005. "The new Latino South: The context and consequences of rapid population growth." http://pewhispanic.org/files/reports/50.1.pdf (accessed November 26, 2010).

Pew Hispanic Center. 2007. "National survey of Latinos: As illegal immigration issue heats up, Hispanics feel a chill." http://pewhispanic.org/files/reports/84.pdf (accessed November 26, 2010).

Pew Research Center. 2006. "America's immigration quandary: No consensus on immigration problem or proposed fixes." http://pewhispanic.org/files/reports/63.pdf (accessed November 26, 2010).

President's commission for the study of ethical problems in medicine and biomedical and behavioral research. 1983. Washington, DC: US Government Printing Office, 131. http://bioethics.georgetown.edu/pcbe/reports/past_commissions/securing_access.pdf (accessed July 16, 2012).

Prindeville, Diane-Michele. 2003. "Identity and the politics of American Indian and Hispanic women leaders." *Gender & Society.* 17 (4): 591–608.

Rich, Adrienne. 2001. "Notes toward a politics of location." In *Arts of the possible: Essays and conversations.* New York: W. W. Norton & Company.

Roberts, Dorothy. 1997. *Killing the Black body: Race, reproduction, and the meaning of liberty.* New York: Pantheon Books.

———. 2002. *Shattered bonds: The color of child welfare.* New York: Basic Civitas Books.

Roediger, David. 1991. *The wages of whiteness: Race and the making of the American working class.* London: Verso.

Rosenbaum, Sara, and Peter Shin. 2003. *Health centers as safety net providers: An overview and assessment of Medicaid's role.* Washington, DC: The Henry J. Kaiser Family Foundation. http://www.kff.org/medicaid/loader.cfm?url=/commonspot/security/getfile.cfm&PageID=14342 (accessed November 26, 2010).

Roth, Benita. 2004. *Separate roads to feminism: Black, Chicana, and white feminist movements in America's second wave.* Cambridge: Cambridge University Press.

Santa Ana, Otto. 2002. *Brown tide rising: Metaphors of Latinos in contemporary American public discourse.* Austin: University of Texas Press.

Sardell, Alice. 1988. *The U.S. experiment in social medicine: The Community Health Center Program, 1965–1986.* Pittsburgh: University of Pittsburgh Press.

Schneider, Joseph. 1985. "Social problems theory: The constructionist view." *Annual Review of Sociology* 11:209–229.

Schwalbe, Michael. 1996. *Unlocking the iron cage: The men's movement, gender politics, and American culture.* New York: Oxford University Press.

———. 2002. "The costs of American privilege." *CounterPunch.* October 4. http://www.counterpunch.org/schwalbe1004.html (accessed November 26, 2010).

———. 2005. *The sociologically examined life: Pieces of the conversation.* Mountain View, CA: Mayfield Publishing Company.

———. 2007. *Rigging the game: How inequality is reproduced in everyday life.* New York: Oxford University Press.

Schwalbe, M., S. Godwin, D. Holden, D. Schrock, S. Thompson, and M. Wolkomir. 2000. "Generic processes in the reproduction of inequality: An interactionist analysis." *Social Forces* 79 (2): 419–452.

Scott, Ellen K. 1998. "Creating partnerships for change: Alliances and betrayals in the racial politics of two feminist organizations." *Gender & Society* 12 (4): 400–423.

———. 2000. "Everyone against racism: Agency and the production of meaning in the anti-racism practices of two feminist organizations." *Theory and Society* 29 (6): 785–818.

Silberman, Pam, Andrea Bazan-Manson, Harriet Purves, Carmen Hooker Odom, Mary P. Easley, Kristie K. Weisner, and Gordon H. DeFries. 2003. "North Carolina Latino health, 2003: A report from the Latino Health Task Force." *North Carolina Medical Journal* 64 (3): 113–121. http://www.ncmedicaljournal.com/wp-content/uploads/NCMJ/may-jun-03/Silberman.pdf (accessed November 26, 2010).

Simonds, Wendy. 1996. *Abortion at work: Ideology and practice in a feminist clinic.* New Brunswick, NJ: Rutgers University Press.

Skaggs, Sheryl, Donald Tomaskovic-Devey, and Jeffrey Leiter. 2000. "Latino/a employment growth in North Carolina: Ethnic displacement or replacement." North Carolina State University. http://sasw.chass.ncsu.edu/jeff/latinos/latino.html (accessed 2009).

Snow, David, and Leon Anderson. 1987. "Identity work among the homeless: The verbal construction and avowal of personal identities." *American Journal of Sociology* 92 (6): 1336–71.

Snow, David, and Robert Benford. 1988. "Ideology, frame resonance, and participant mobilization." *International Social Movement Research* 1:197–217.

Solinger, Rickie. 2000. *Wake up Little Susie: Single pregnancy and race before Roe v. Wade*, 2nd ed. New York: Routledge.

Staiti, Andrea B., Robert E. Hurley, and Aaron Katz. 2006. *Stretching the safety net to serve undocumented immigrants: Community responses to health needs.* Washington DC: Center for Studying Health System Change. http://www .hschange.org/CONTENT/818/ (accessed November 24, 2010).

Stein, Michael. 1989. "Gratitude and attitude: A note on emotional welfare." *Social Psychology Quarterly* 52 (3): 242–248.

Summers, Keyonna. 2006. "Blacks see threat from Hispanic illegal aliens." *Washington Times*, May 15. http://nl.newsbank.com/nl-search/we/Archives?p_product=WT&p_theme=wt&p_action=search&p_maxdocs=200&p_text_search-0=blacks%20AND%20see%20AND%20threat%20AND%20from%20AND%20Hispanic%20AND%20illegal%20AND%20aliens&s_dispstring=blacks%20see%20threat%20from%20Hispanic%20illegal%20aliens%20AND%20date(2006)&p_field_date-0=YMD_date&p_params_date-0=date:B,E&p_text_date-0=2006&p_perpage=10&p_sort=YMD_date:D&xcal_useweights=no (accessed November 24, 2010).

Swidler, Ann. 1986. "Culture in action: Symbols and strategies." *American Sociological Review* 51 (2): 273–86.

Tatum, Beverly Daniel. 2003. *"Why are all the Black kids sitting together in the cafeteria?" and other conversations about race.* New York: Basic Books.

Taylor, Verta. 1999. "Gender and social movements: Gender processes in women's self-help movements." *Gender & Society* 13:8–33.

Taylor, Verta, and Nancy E. Whittier. 1992. "Collective identity in social movement communities: Lesbian feminist mobilization." In *Frontiers in social movement theory*, edited by A. D. Morris and C. M. Mueller, 76–87. New Haven, CT: Yale University Press.

Tong, Rosemarie Putnam. 1998. *Feminist thought: A more comprehensive introduction.* Boulder, CO: Westview Press.

US Census Bureau. 2010. North Carolina quick facts from the US Census Bureau. State and County Quick Facts. http://quickfacts.census.gov/qfd/states/37000.html (accessed June 23, 2012).

US Census Bureau Poverty Report. 2000. www.census.gov/prod/2001pubs/p60-214.pdf (accessed November 24, 2010).

US Census Data. 2008. http://factfinder.census.gov/servlet/ADPTable?_bm=y&-geo_id=16000US3711800&-qr_name=ACS_2008_3YR_G00_DP3YR5&-ds_name=ACS_2008_3YR_G00_&-_lang=en&-_sse=on (accessed November 19, 2010).

US Department of Health and Human Services. 2005. "Overview of the uninsured in the United States: An analysis of the 2005 current population survey." Assistant Secretary for Planning and Evaluation Issue Brief. http://aspe.hhs.gov/health/reports/05/uninsured-cps/ib.pdf (accessed November 24, 2010).

Waldinger, Roger, and Michael Lichter. 2003. *How the other half works: Immigration and the social organization of labor.* Berkeley and Los Angeles: University of California Press.

Wall, Glenda. 2001. "Moral constructions of motherhood in breastfeeding discourse." *Gender & Society* 15 (4): 592–610.

Wellman, David T. 1993. *Portraits of white racism.* New York: Cambridge University Press.

Williams, Lucy A. 1995. "Race, rat bites and unfit mothers: How media discourse informs welfare legislation debate." *Fordham Urban Law Journal* 22:1159–96.

Williams, Norma, and Minerva Correa. 2003. "Race and ethnic relations." In *Handbook of symbolic interaction,* edited by Larry T. Reynolds and Nancy J. Herman-Kinney, 743–760. Walnut Creek, CA: Alta Mira Press.

Wilson, William Julius. 1978. *The declining significance of race: Blacks and changing American institutions.* Chicago: University of Chicago Press.

———. 1987. *The truly disadvantaged: The inner city, the underclass, and public policy.* Chicago: University of Chicago Press.

———. 1996. *When work disappears: The world of the new urban poor.* New York: Alfred A. Knopf.

Winant, Howard. 2004. *The new politics of race: Globalism, difference, justice.* Minneapolis: University of Minnesota Press.

WRAL.com. 2005. "In-state tuition bill misses key N.C. legislative deadline." June 7. http://www.wral.com/news/local/story/1090928/ (accessed November 24, 2010).

Zúñiga, Víctor, and Rubén Hernández-León, eds. 2005. *New destinations: Mexican immigration in the United States.* New York: Russell Sage Foundation.

Index

About the Author

NATALIA DEEB-SOSSA, an assistant professor in the University of California at Davis' Chicana/o Studies Department, has conducted research in medical sociology, social psychology, symbolic interaction, methodology, and race, class, and gender. All of her work makes contributions to substantive issues in inequality. In her dissertation, through participant observation and in-depth interviews, Natalia analyzed how workers at a private, not-for-profit health care center reproduce—or resist reproducing—inequalities of race, class, and gender in their interactions with each other and in their daily work with the poor, especially Latinas/os. These inequalities are examined in a setting where health care providers face competing goals, conflicting demands, and understaffing.

Her current research focuses on women's reproductive rights; Mexican women's access to health care via formal (institutional) and informal (cultural) avenues; study of curanderas, parteras, and yerberas; sources of health care for sexually transmitted infections (STIs); family planning and abortion; and health care issues with Mexican migrant agricultural workers.